Praise for
Advice That Sticks

Finally, someone is willing to tackle the complex issue of client compliance and how change occurs in the area of personal and business finance. Written by an expert in the field of financial psychology, the book delivers humility, humor and wisdom. It guides the reader in learning how to close the gap between good intentions and actions.

Courtney Pullen, M.A.
Author, *Intentional Wealth*

This is a great book! A worn and dog-eared copy belongs on the bookshelf of every financial advisor who views financial planning as a calling and a profession.

Rick Kahler, MSFP, CFP®
Author, *Conscious Finance*

Consumers know they need to do things differently with respect to their money, but are often dismayed or baffled by their own self-sabotaging habits. Financial professionals have not always known how to be helpful in creating lasting behaviour change. They've relied too much on the provision of information and the occasional stern lecture. This book will change all that. It is superbly written, and well-positioned to help a lot of people.

Kelley Keehn
Finance author & consumer advocate

Dr. Moira Somers has given professional advisors an inspired gift in *Advice That Sticks*. She shares dozens of adherence-boosting strategies, including outstanding recommended questions to ask clients. I love Somers' delightfully dry humor, which sparkles throughout! This book's insightful, disciplined, evidence-based process will enhance advisors' effectiveness as advice-givers.

Kathleen Rehl, Ph.D., CFP®, CeFT®
Author, *Moving Forward on Your Own*

With this book, every financial professional has access to deeply practical advice on how to listen, observe and respond while helping clients make their best life and money decisions. This is the book that connects financial planners and wealth advisors with the human experience of decision-making, commitments and adaptation to change.

Susan Bradley, CFP®
Founder, Sudden Money Institute

Financial professionals need to understand their clients' values, attitudes and beliefs about money, emotions, biases and social influences, and then connect with their clients with in a way that motivates and facilitates the right outcomes. This book highlights the importance of these skills along with Moira's helpful insights and guidance for providing advice that sticks.

Joan Yudelson, CFP®
VP, Professional Practice,
Financial Planning Standards Council

ADVICE
THAT
STICKS

HOW TO GIVE FINANCIAL ADVICE
THAT PEOPLE WILL FOLLOW

MOIRA SOMERS, PH.D.

First published in Great Britain by Practical Inspiration
Publishing, 2018

© Moira Somers, 2018

The moral rights of the author have been asserted

All case studies have been anonymized and no real names
have been used.

ISBN (print): 978-1-78860-014-9
ISBN (ebook): 978-1-78860-015-6 (Kindle)
ISBN (ebook): 978-1-78860-021-7 (epub)

 Practical Inspiration
PUBLISHING

For Jean-Louis

All these years later, I'm still so happy to be stuck with you!

Contents

Introduction

Here's what I've come to believe: Most people are at least mildly crazy when it comes to money.

I can say 'crazy' with some authority. I am, after all, a psychologist. I know crazy when I see it. And there is nothing – not full moons or federal elections or family get-togethers – that draws the crazy out of people faster than money.

The author Geneen Roth describes it more eloquently:

It seems that money, even more than food, activates our survival instinct and makes wise, otherwise rational people behave like starving dogs. Any distorted or frozen patterns in our psyches will inevitably show up in our relationship with money, which makes it the ultimate repository for shadowy behavior.

Geneen Roth, *Lost and Found*

Craziness. Starving dogs. Shadowy behaviour. So ... are you *sure* you want to work with people and their money?

If your work involves giving people financial counsel, then their crazy, conflicted relationship to money is only one of the challenges you will face. Frankly, it's not even the most formidable one. Factors such as the quality of your relationship with clients, their level of energy and insight, and a host of other social and environmental influences all contribute mightily to what the client will do with the recommendations you provide.

Unfortunately, the odds are high that you have not received much guidance on what to actually *do* about any of these other influences. As a financial professional, the bulk of your training and expertise lies in highly technical domains. You know the ins and outs of taxation, pensions, investment vehicles and insurance options. You are savvy about key market indicators and the interpretation of financial data. You know a great deal about the ethics and laws governing your professional activities. You know all about the best products and services to help people reach their goals.

But most financial professionals* receive very little training in client psychology, and in the related art and science of *giving* advice. Advice that is timely, palatable, and easy for clients to understand. Advice that is custom-designed not only to be technically sound, but also to be 'just right' in terms of the client's ability to receive and act upon it.

This book fills the gap in that training. I want you to be able to give financial advice in such a way that three things happen:

1. your *great recommendations are followed* by your clients,
2. your *clients' well-being is maximized* as a result, and
3. you experience a *massive boost in your career success and satisfaction.*

---

* This book is written for anyone who gives professional counsel to people regarding how to deal with money matters. This includes Certified Financial Planners®, accountants, estate attorneys, bankers, business consultants and credit counsellors. Financial therapists and money coaches will also find much that is germane to their work. I will frequently use the noun "advisor" throughout this book, but I use it in the generic sense of "one who gives advice".

Throughout this book, I will be sharing evidence-based, practical tips with you. These are strategies that have emerged from decades of research into two intriguing questions. The first: What makes it so hard for people to do the right things for their well-being? The second: What can be done to help them make lasting, meaningful changes in their behaviour?

Most of the earliest studies in this regard were targeted at health-related behaviours (things like quitting smoking or taking medication properly). The scope of the studies has expanded greatly since then. Broader applications of research findings have had a transformative impact on fields as varied as environmental protection and elite-level sports performance. It is high time for such a transformation to take place within the financial professions.

For the past decade, I have been adapting these strategies to help bring about lasting, meaningful change in the lives of the clients I see in my own work as a financial psychologist and executive coach. The approaches have been further field-tested and tweaked by the financial professionals I consult with around the globe. I am confident that you, like them, will find that these easy-to-implement strategies make a world of difference in your clients' willingness and ability to follow your advice.

By the end of this book, you will know how to give *advice that sticks*. And perhaps – just perhaps – you might also find that you have been able to address some of your own areas of stubborn resistance to change. So read on to find out what an agitated professor and a wounded lumberjack have in common; how empathy, confidence, and blueberries can all be dangerous; and what my mother being branded a tart has to do with anything at all.

Two kinds of expertise are needed

Throughout this book, I will be making a distinction between the *technical* and the *personal* sides of advising. The technical side has to do with the domain-specific financial knowledge that you are examined upon throughout your education and credentialing journey (e.g. taxation, investment strategies, cash flow projections). The personal side has to do with client psychology and life situation (e.g. goals, abilities, energy level, outlook, family dynamics). 'Both sides are equally complex and equally important,' maintains Susan Bradley, founder of the Sudden Money® Institute and a thought leader in the financial advising profession. Regrettably, most credentialing programmes in the financial professions seem to operate on the assumption that, once the technical stuff is mastered, the so-called 'soft skills' will take care of themselves.

When it comes to clients not following through with recommendations, it's rarely because the advisor is technically unskilled or incorrect. Instead, it's usually because the personal side of things has been neglected or misread. If you've been working with people and their money for any length of time, you will likely have come to the conclusion that the technical side of advising is comparatively easy. It's the 'soft' side that's the hard side!

Many financial service professionals have realized they need a different kind of training, one that addresses human psychology. Organizations such as the Kinder Institute, Money Quotient, Sudden Money® Institute, and Financial Recovery Institute have spearheaded the delivery of excellent specialized training in this regard. Interdisciplinary collaboratives and think tanks such as the Purposeful Planning Institute and the Nazrudin Project have offered further opportunities for a broad range of professionals to come together, reflect on money's meaning and effects, and influence the evolution of their respective disciplines. *Advice that Sticks* merges the teachings of these pioneering financial deep thinkers with the scientific literature on non-adherence and behaviour change.

Need, opportunity and gift

This book is for any advisor who understands the NEED, the OPPORTUNITY, and the GIFT that exist with respect to delivering advice more skilfully.

Level 1: Need

You know the irony of this situation as well as I do. In an era when financial guidance has never been easier to obtain, the citizenry of the developed world has dismal savings levels and record amounts of indebtedness. Yet none of the branches of the financial services industry seem to be taking into account the fundamental complexity of human psychology. They just keep on telling people the same old messages about what they should be doing, as though more telling will result in more uptake.

The evidence by now is pretty clear that this is not a knowledge problem; it's an implementation problem. It's not unlike knowing that apples are better for us than chips, even as we reach into the bag for more salty, fatty yumminess. What we need instead of more information is more help in bridging the gap between correct knowledge and effective action.

This need exists, not just for the betterment of our clients' lives, but also for the future of the various financial professions. Huge shake-ups are taking place industry-wide, but especially within the specific domain of financial planning. Faceless, interchangeable robo-advisors are taking on a bigger share of the market, and mature advisory firms are seeing slowing rates of client acquisition. The financial advising profession is having trouble attracting new recruits.

Across the broader financial services industry (which includes banks, insurance companies, brokerages, investment funds, and credit card companies), unsavoury and hidden practices are coming to the attention of the public. Legislative changes are being enacted worldwide that will increase transparency with respect to such things as disclosure of fees and debt servicing costs. These numbers are now staring consumers in the face with every credit card bill or investment statement that arrives in the mailbox. In response, consumers are becoming more assertive with service providers, insisting that they prove their worth, lower their fees, or lose the business. As a financial services professional, you need to focus on adding value to the advising relationship itself, as the profit margins for financial products or technical expertise alone will continue to be squeezed.

Level 2: Opportunity

Hidden within any threat or challenge you might be facing are the seeds of opportunity:

> If you have been losing clients or assets under management, you have an opportunity to understand and reverse that trend.

If you have been longing to develop a stable, enthusiastic roster of clients that you can serve for life, there is an opportunity for you to develop expertise in client psychology that will be a strong differentiator from your competitors.

If you are curious about the burgeoning fields of neuroeconomics, positive psychology, and behavioural economics, there is an opportunity to capitalize on the exploding body of knowledge that is emerging to help shape desired behaviour change.

By embracing the challenge, you can base your work on a more complex, nuanced understanding of what it is *to be* and *to advise* a human investor and consumer. Odds are high that you will also end up lowering your own stress level and that of your team, because you won't constantly be stymied and frustrated by clients who are not following through.

Level 3: Gift

Much has been written about the different attitudes people hold towards their work. Some view what they do merely as a *job*; others see it as part of a desirable *career*; still others, as a sacred *calling*. I have had the distinct honour of working with financial professionals who show up to their work each day as though it were a calling. They are the ones who get invited to walk alongside their clients on some of the best and hardest days of their lives.

Perhaps you are among them. If so, you know that such experiences are truly a gift. There is a feeling of being on sacred ground when a client shares a deeply held value or discloses a profoundly moving event from the past. It is a powerful thing to be one of the first people trusted to receive news of a pending birth, a big business merger, or a serious diagnosis. And it can be deeply satisfying to know you've been instrumental in helping some clients get back on their feet after setbacks, and in helping others stay grounded when they have grown overly exuberant.

How does that happen? How does one both receive and impart such professional gifts? It happens to advisors who have equipped themselves to be 'Thinking Partners' with their clients, co-creators of action plans that solve problems and facilitate goal achievement. Such advisors rarely give one-size-fits-all solutions, leaving the client to tug and yank at the advice until it (sort of) fits them; rather, they take the time to find out the clients' needs and motivations and misgivings, and tailor their advice accordingly. My hope is that, as a result of reading this book, you will be inspired and equipped to make the changes needed for you to become a true Thinking Partner for your clients.

But it's possible you won't. That's because the same things that make it hard for your clients to implement your great recommendations will make it hard for you to implement mine. Doing things differently is hard, especially if you try to do too much at once, on your own, or without any systems in place to remind you of the changes you're trying to make. I've had more than a few such experiences, myself.

How I was undone by a blueberry

Several years ago, a prolonged bout of low energy led me to embark on a whole-health makeover. I hired a personal trainer; I started taking vitamin supplements; I began exercising more often and getting to bed earlier. And it worked! Within mere weeks, I started feeling more energetic ... and maybe a little too ambitious. I decided to move on to better eating habits.

It was a time when antioxidants were all the rage, the key to eternal life and world peace. I was convinced that eating a daily dose of fresh berries would turn me into a force of nature. And that's when it all came crashing down ... because getting those fresh berries meant remembering to buy them, and buying them meant making a few more trips to the supermarket every week. That, in turn, required a couple more episodes a week of stuffing the kids into their snowsuits, and wrestling them into their car seats. Soon the whole self-improvement gig just fell off the radar. I'd tried to change too much, too fast, and as a result I ended up changing very little of anything.

How to use this book

Be wary of the Blueberry Effect, good reader! Here are some ideas to help you detour around that trap and head straight for glory:

1. As you go through the book, be sure to look over the Adherence Boosters listed at the end of the chapter (from Chapter 2 onwards). Highlight any of the recommendations that seem particularly germane to you and/or your team.

2. Once you've reached the end of the book, perform a triage on those highlighted areas. Identify the top two

to three areas of greatest need or promise. Note that many of the changes simply involve adding in a question or two to your client meetings, but they will require dogged, consistent application to see results.

3. Choose just one of those areas to work on for the next month. Write down what you plan to do differently, and why. Tell someone else about what you are committing to do. Put a note in your calendar every 30 days to check in on how you've been doing and to identify what you want to tackle next.

4. Find a way to keep those change intentions top of mind. I have a practice of e-mailing myself several questions at the start of each day, reminding myself of the existing habits I'd like to maintain (e.g. emptying my inbox) and the emerging habits I'm striving to establish (e.g. practising music for 20 minutes a day). This keeps earnest but fragile resolutions from falling into the abyss.

5. Every time you try out a new strategy, give yourself credit. Notice what went well, and what needs further alteration or customization.

6. Whenever possible, enlist someone else in the cause. See if there are some advice-enhancing practices that you and a colleague would like to work on at the same time.

7. Each month, when prompted, review your progress. Determine whether you're ready to embrace another strategy for giving advice that won't go to waste. Then repeat the above steps.

8. If you'd like to develop your expertise even further
   in the personal side of advising, or look into getting
   additional training or coaching, drop me a line at
   drsomers@moneymindandmeaning.com – I'd be happy
   to help.

Chapter 1

The Value of Advice That Sticks

It's shocking, really

Every day in my work as a financial psychologist, I am reminded of Van de Graaff static-electricity generators, those basketball-sized metal globes that are a regular fixture in physics labs and science museums. Reach out your hand and touch them, and your hair rises up in a sphere all around your head. I have found that money, for most people, acts in a similar way. It carries an incredible emotional charge.

What else would explain the weird things that financial professionals encounter in their line of work? There's the gazillionaire business owner, howling with outrage over an $8 courier charge for the last-minute documents she demanded from her accountant. There's the dumbfounded overspender, staring at the bankruptcy application the credit counsellor warned he'd be facing if he didn't rein in his spending. There's the fighting couple, arguing about whose idea it was to hide their income from the government, and looking to their financial planner to both referee and rescue them from the consequences.

Just as you can only see the results of electricity (and not electricity itself), so it is that you can only see the results of people's emotions and beliefs around money. It shows up in their spending habits, job choices, and relationships. It shows up in their investment decisions and in their charitable giving. It shows up in the tone and the content of the conversations they have with you and other people in their life when money gets discussed. One of the challenges you face as a financial advisor is how to work with the financial equivalent of live electrical wires. How do you do your work without getting 'zapped' by those hidden emotional charges that can thwart the best of advice?

You are uniquely positioned to be the ground wire for clients with emotionally charged financial histories. Doing so requires a firm commitment to not add to the problem through shaming, blaming, or firing them unnecessarily. You are more likely to succeed at this if you have examined the people and events that have influenced your own financial values and beliefs over your lifetime. You also need to ensure that you're not a financial 'live wire', yourself!

Good advice that's hard to take

As a species, humans can be an ornery lot. When faced with complex decisions, we want advice about what is the right thing to do, and generally we want to do it. Except, of course, for those times when we'd rather do something else. Something easier. Something more understandable. Something more fun. Regrettably, *something else* seems to crop up with surprising frequency when it comes to money.

Helping people do sensible things with their money is just as hard as getting people to do the right things for their health. As a result, financial professionals can feel like the spoilsports at the party of life, urging prudence and moderation while the fun guys are rolling out the kegs of beer and trays of nachos. In addition to its tendency towards dullness, prudent financial advice has the problem of being radically counter-culture. Think about it. Aside from the professions of health care and finance, what other secular forces in society routinely promote self-restraint and long-term thinking instead of immediate gratification? I'll tell you this with some confidence: 1-click ordering was not invented by a financial advisor!

Good advice that's unskilfully given

If financial professionals are already fighting an uphill battle because of the nature of the advice they give and the broader culture in which they are giving it, then their lack of training in the *personal* side of their trade surely makes the battle that much harder. They make preventable mistakes, including the following ones:

Assuming that people who solicit and pay for their advice are ready to take action.

Using incomprehensible jargon.

Disregarding the emotional side of the client experience.

Being blindsided by predictable problems in follow-through.

Overestimating how much people are capable of taking on when they're undergoing major life transitions.

Acting as though the client lives in a social vacuum.

Allowing disapproval, disappointment or disdain to taint the relationship.

Many years ago, medical training was in the same state that most fields of financial training are in today. One oft-cited survey of physicians in the 1970s found that only 25% of them acknowledged the possibility that they had anything to do with patient non-compliance.[1] The emphasis was entirely on the *technical correctness* of the advice given to patients. But all too often, patient non-compliance undermined any hope that the otherwise excellent medical advice would improve clinical outcomes.

Although patient-blaming has long been a beloved pastime for doctors and nurses, eventually a critical mass of people grew tired of the sport. Discerning eyes were turned towards the medical schools. Professors were challenged to explain what good was being served in teaching students how to select the correct hypertensive or antibiotic if the prescription never was purchased or taken properly. Or where the value was in teaching state-of-the-art surgical techniques if the patient failed to do post-surgical exercises or make important lifestyle changes. And so it was that research began in earnest about how to deal with non-compliant patients. There are now four decades of studies that have dug deeply into this problem.

The results have been rather startling. It turns out that the problem lies as much with the advice-giver and with the nature of the advice itself as it does with the advice-taker. The archetypal 'non-compliant' client does not, in truth, exist.

A sticky problem – or, rather, a problem of stickiness

As a result of such findings, the very terminology used to describe the problem has changed. Medical professionals are encouraged to use the term 'non-adherence' rather than 'non-compliance'. The former is seen as being less judgmental, not as entrenched in the power differential between doctor and patient.

Ironically, there has been a lot of non-adherence in the medical community around the use of the word 'non-adherence'! I understand the reluctance to change words. The term itself is a little awkward. 'Non-adherence' sounds less like a human problem and more like a manufacturing challenge for the glue industry. ('Hey boss – this self-adhesive wallpaper isn't very adherent.' 'Yeah, I know. That's a special run sponsored by divorce lawyers.')

Over time, the term 'non-adherence' has grown on me. I like the mental association with stickiness. It helps me avoid the all-too-easy path of exasperated client-blaming – 'Why won't she just LISTEN to me?' – and nudges me to consider a broader view of the problem: namely, that the advice is not 'sticky' enough, and that the client and I need to figure out what we could do about that.

But there's been more than just a change in terminology. The field of adherence research has led to a revamping of medical education. Since the 1980s, students have been taught to consider why certain advice is harder to take than other kinds, and what would make it easier for patients to do the right thing under difficult conditions. Lectures on this topic – and even entire courses – are now embedded into the curricula of medical schools and mental health training programmes. Adherence research informs virtually every aspect of primary medical care as well as preventative health campaigns and rehabilitation efforts.

Financial advisor training, alas, has not kept pace with this field of knowledge. One advisor lamented to me, 'The only advice I got with respect to 'soft skills' was to have a firm handshake and to use mouthwash.'

Well, that's a start, I guess.

A broader perspective

For the purposes of this book, adherence will be broadly defined as *the extent to which a person's actions align with agreed-upon recommendations from practitioners*. Note the element of co-creation that exists in this approach: The recommendations must be *agreed upon*.

This broader perspective comes from no less august an organization than the World Health Organization. In 2003, the WHO issued an influential report outlining five main factors that influence such alignment.[2] As I began moving from my work as a neuropsychologist in health care into the emerging fields of financial psychology and behavioural economics, I saw that the same five factors were at work in influencing the likelihood of adherence to financial advice.

Throughout this book, I will be using the acronym FACTS to help you remember those five main contributors to financial adherence. The following graphic shows what those dimensions are, moving clockwise from the top:

The sections below provide just a brief summary of how each of the five domains influences the likelihood of follow-through with your advice.

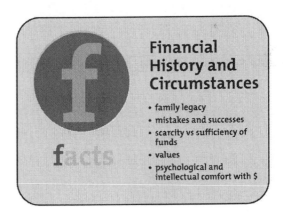

Financial History and Circumstances: The specific domain of finance has associated challenges that are not seen in other fields. Clients come to you with a lifetime of individual and collective experiences with money, experiences that have contributed to their sense of relative financial competence and confidence. The challenges in this domain include dealing with factors largely internal to the client (e.g. family legacies, personal values, financial literacy) as well as external realities (e.g. access to funds, market cycles, changing life circumstances).

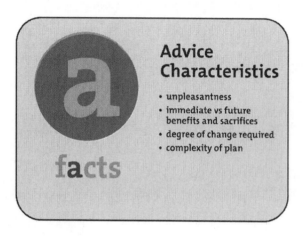

Advice Characteristics: No matter what area of behaviour change we might be considering, there will be certain features of the advice that will influence people's willingness to follow it. Adherence is greatly affected by such things as the pleasantness or complexity of the tasks we prescribe, the time requirements for implementation, and any associated need to delay gratification. As you will learn, much financial advice can be hard to swallow because of some of these general advice characteristics.

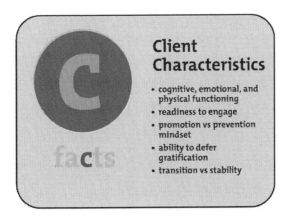

Client
Characteristics

• cognitive, emotional, and physical functioning
• readiness to engage
• promotion vs prevention mindset
• ability to defer gratification
• transition vs stability

Client Characteristics: The same piece of advice that one client finds easy to implement may require gargantuan effort from another. This is because of differences in such things as energy levels, motivation, outlook, and intellectual abilities. By understanding such influences and tailoring your advice accordingly, you can play a large role in ensuring that clients are truly ready to begin and to persist with their change attempts.

Team and
Advisor Factors

• language complexity
• support for implementation
• warmth/empathy vs judgement/disdain
• frequency of follow-up
• processes to handle impasses

Team and Advisor Factors: How you behave with clients will have a direct bearing on their receptivity to your recommendations. By learning about such things as the need to reduce language complexity, listen more attentively, and relate with greater warmth and less judgment, you and your team will come to understand the critical role you play in increasing adherence.

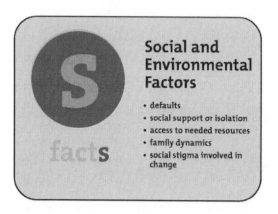

Social and Environmental Factors: Our clients do not function in a vacuum – they are part of a complex social and cultural network that greatly influences their behaviour, often to a far greater degree than we do. It is important for both client and advisor to try and identify such influences so that they can be harnessed or mitigated accordingly.

Each one of these five dimensions of adherence exerts its own influence on follow-through, but none of them exists in isolation. Each domain interacts with the others, increasing or decreasing the likelihood that your clients will act in alignment with agreed-upon recommendations. In real-world practice, then, the FACTS model of adherence looks less like a uni-directional clock, and more like a spider web or a dream catcher:

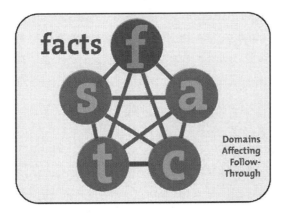

There is a tendency for professionals from all walks of life to place heavy emphasis on the factual correctness of their advice, and to then blame the client when things don't happen. The FACTS model corrects that unhelpful oversimplification. My hope is that you will return to this diagram with a spirit of curiosity and openness any time that you encounter adherence challenges in the future.

Refuse to be surprised

Upon learning that I am a psychologist, it is not uncommon for people to say something along the lines of, 'I bet there's nothing that surprises you anymore about people.' Oh, yes there is! Two decades into this line of work, I am still routinely gobsmacked by the ridiculous, tender, grasping, harsh and thoughtful things our species is capable of. But the one thing that does NOT surprise me anymore is the difficulty all people have in bridging the gap between their good intentions and the actions that will accomplish their aims.

The authors of *Changing for Good*[3] (a classic book on behaviour change) claim that, at any given time, only 20% of us are ready to bridge that intention–action gap. That is, only one in five people who freely admit to having a problem is truly committed to taking corrective action on it in the immediate future. Once this minority begins the journey towards goal achievement or problem resolution, they are usually then beset by additional challenges that further reduce the likelihood of success. With this in mind, then, *non-adherence is best understood as the norm, not the exception.* From here on in, you, too, should refuse to be surprised by the emergence of non-adherence; in fact, you should anticipate it, in order to head it off at the pass.

Advantages of giving advice that sticks

Why is it important for you to get better at helping people complete an agreed-upon course of action?

There are the obvious client-relevant reasons:

1. If they don't adhere to the plan, clients may court some serious troubles: impoverished retirements, family disputes, legal troubles, bankruptcy, etc.
2. When they do adhere, clients are more able to reach deeply cherished goals: seeing the world, making charitable contributions, moving out of their parents' basement.
3. Clients' self-esteem and sense of integrity are diminished when they don't keep their promises. Non-adherent

clients frequently become dispirited and embarrassed by their lack of action.

4. Clients who feel bad about themselves and their lack of follow-through are less likely to attend subsequent appointments or comply with additional requests. They often go AWOL and fade silently away. Non-adherence begets non-adherence.

Then there are the factors that more directly affect the advisor:

5. Adherent clients have lower drop-out rates. It is much less work to keep existing clients for the long term than it is to have to continually recruit new ones.

6. Non-adherent clients can pose logistical, relational, or even legal problems for an advisor. They require more frequent phone calls and e-mails to nudge them along; they call more often in a panic (once their procrastination has reached crisis proportions) and demand immediate attention; they miss key deadlines and fail to provide legally required documentation.

7. Clients who are positively engaged with their own financial plans tend to be more satisfied clients who refer friends and family members. Non-engaged clients rarely do so. Non-adherence thereby has very real financial implications for the advisor.

8. Advisor satisfaction increases when clients are keeping their commitments, and decreases when they're not. Let's be honest about this: Some clients take a toll on us. They leave us feeling stressed, inadequate, worried,

and frustrated. In the words of the American spiritual writer Anne Lamott, such clients are enough to 'make Jesus want to drink gin straight out of the cat dish'. The more effective we can become in helping clients make important changes and avoid regrettable actions, the more we're doing for our own well-being. (Plus, the cat gets to keep its dish. Everybody wins.)

And finally, there are regulatory issues:

9.　As I write this book, the Fiduciary Standard is poised to become the standard of the financial planning profession in many jurisdictions. This standard brings with it not just the *duty of loyalty* but also the *duty of care*. Advisors will be obliged to demonstrate that the advice they give is, first and foremost, *competent* advice. While there are bound to be disputes over what, exactly, constitutes competence in advice giving, there can be little doubt that it will have to include elements of being tailored to the individual, of being understandable, and of taking into account all aspects of the client's life circumstances. These elements of competence are also key elements of adherence.

10. Helping people reach their goals is what we're being paid to do; therefore, taking money from people who are not fulfilling their part of the bargain has implications for our continued work with them. Financial services author and editor Bob Veres argues that we have an ethical obligation to end the advisor–client relationship

when the client is chronically unable or unwilling to carry out recommended actions.[4]

Good advice, skilfully delivered

Advice-giving is a complex skill all on its own, one that merits training all of its own. That's what this book aims to deliver. *Giving good advice well* requires three things of us: (1) that we understand and harness our clients' motivation and concerns; (2) that we help provide them with clear direction on how to reach their goals; and (3) that we have a plan for dealing with the inevitable obstacles that will crop up along the way.

There are a few assumptions that undergird this book. The first assumption is that your advice is technically sound. A second is that your advice is ethically beyond reproach. A third is that your technically correct, ethically impeccable counsel is a good fit for the situations of your particular clients. Put somewhat differently:

Some advice is bad. That, I can't help you with.
Some advice is badly given. That, I can.

So let's dig in. But first, take a break and go use some mouthwash. (It's really not a bad place to start.)

Chapter 2

Why People Seek Advice

Throughout this book, we'll be considering the question of why people frequently fail to implement excellent financial advice – the kind of advice that has the potential to benefit lives, permanently and profoundly. But before we dive into those troubled waters, we'd be wise to back up a few steps and consider a more fundamental question: What leads people to seek your advice in the first place?

The question is so fundamental that it often gets overlooked. Getting in touch with the answers can transform how you show up for your clients. It can tell you when to put a relative emphasis on *client experience* versus *technical expertise* at differing points of contact with them. Not incidentally, it can also be used to guide your marketing efforts, making sure that they're targeted at the issues of concern to your potential clients.

Your own reasons for seeking advice

Think of some recent times that you reached out for some counsel. What were you hoping for?

Maybe you needed to confirm something you had already investigated: *I think this repair is covered by the warranty. Can you verify that for me?*

Or it could have been that you were looking for solutions to a longstanding dilemma: *How can I get my dog to stop jumping on people?*

Or perhaps you were stuck with a number of complex options that were all emotionally wrenching: *What would you do if it were YOUR dad showing signs of dementia?*

Or maybe you just needed a perspective that you couldn't get on your own: *Does my butt look big in this muumuu?*

Whatever the particulars, you asked for advice because *you wanted help in solving a problem.* The help you were seeking may have come in one of many forms: information, guidance, reassurance, etc. If that advice met your needs, you left the encounter with a better knowledge of what action to take, what decision to make. If the encounter was helpful, you would have been left with greater confidence and calm. But if that advice did not help you solve your problem, you would have left the encounter feeling just as dissatisfied or unsettled as when you started – or even, unhappily, more so.

Having an unsolved problem creates a state of mental tension; solving the problem allows the individual to return to a state of psychological equilibrium or homeostasis. Returning to a settled state just feels better, plain and simple. Such quietening or settling can occur even when people are asking for help that seemingly has no emotional import whatsoever, and even when they end up rejecting the advice they've been given. (We'll delve into this paradox in a subsequent chapter.)

But remember this: *All decisions have an emotional component to them.* People seek advice to solve a problem so that they can feel more settled.

The wisdom of the collective

Reflect again on your own recent experiences of advice-seeking. Chances are you reached out for advice because you believed it would lead to a quicker, better, more satisfactory outcome than you could achieve on your own. And chances are you would have been correct in that belief. The quality of people's decision-making is often demonstrably better when they consult with other people.

One of the highest-rated game shows in television history is the international phenomenon, *Who Wants to be a Millionaire?* The game requires contestants to answer a series of multiple-choice questions of varying difficulty. Any wrong answer results in immediate ejection from the show. When they're stumped by a question, contestants on that game show have a one-time option of polling the studio audience, and then deciding whether to go with the majority answer or strike out on their own.

I've often wondered how much help could be offered to contestants by an audience made up of people from all walks of life. The questions run the gamut from science to history to entertainment and beyond – it's like a high-stakes version of Trivial Pursuit. So how useful are the collective guesses of a non-expert audience? In their fascinating book, *Sway: The Irresistible Pull of Irrational Behaviour*, authors Ori and Rom Brafman were able to put an end to my wondering. According to the Brafmans, the audience is correct 90% of the time. That's far better than the odds the befuddled contestants start out with.

Asking for guidance from a relatively random group of non-expert strangers makes sense if you're in a time-pressured, do-or-die situation on national television.* Blessedly, that is a rare event. Most of the time, we're able to be more discerning about the people we reach out to. That's a good thing, because the decisions we face are usually a good deal more complex. The answers we seek are not so much cut-and-dried factual ones; they tend to be more nuanced and personalized than that. Nevertheless, the take-home message remains: If we're looking to make the best possible decisions for our lives, other people are often our best and most important resource.

The common ground of financial experts and tattoo artists

Why do people seek *your* advice? What is it that people are hoping to get from *you*, the expert? Until quite recently, the answer would have included *access to a product or a body of knowledge not available elsewhere.*

There was a time when financial experts had unique and privileged access to the tools and expertise of their trade. If

---

* But not everywhere. Asking for help from the audience in Russia or France is not a good strategy, according to the Brafmans. Cultural norms there render it more likely that they'll deliberately give contestants the wrong answers. Tuck that little piece of information away for future reference, just in case you're ever on a game show in Moscow or Paris.

folks wanted to buy insurance, stocks, bonds, or mutual funds, they needed someone to do it for them. This was true of pretty much every profession and trade prior to the mid-1990s. Training and credentials gave experts an exclusive 'lock' on such things as procedural training, trade publications, and purchasing and sales rights. Regulatory guidelines helped ensure that knowledge was protected within each profession's particular guild. It was all proprietary – for tattoo artists and stockbrokers, for welders and insurance salespeople.

Technology has changed all that. With every day that passes, the amount of secret or proprietary information shrinks, and what is considered 'public domain' grows. Access to knowledge and products or supplies is steadily being democratized. Want to know the brand of knickers favoured by the Queen? Keen to discover how to get slugs off your lettuce plants? Need access to a trading platform so you can buy some penny mining stocks? It's all available in seconds with some clicks of a mouse.

I'm not meaning to be indelicate here, but given the above-mentioned changes, the question needs to be asked: *What good are you, anyway?* Well, a lot of good, as it turns out. Let's turn to the reasons consumers give when asked why they turn to experts – financial and otherwise.

Why consumers turn to the experts

As you read through the following aims that consumers have in seeking help, give some thought to how you might integrate this knowledge into both your marketing and promotion efforts as well as your service delivery.

To reduce complexity

Because of an inherent belief that *more knowledge = better decision making*, many people now make a point of gathering copious amounts of information on the problem they're trying to solve. It is not uncommon for customers and clients to show up with tomes of research they've gathered, eager to discuss their findings. But the gathering of information does not automatically turn consumers into experts, particularly when the domain is highly technical and complex. (Just ask any physician who has had to tangle with a patient armed with WebMD diagnoses and treatment possibilities.)

What true experts are able to do is judge the credibility and utility of the available information in order to separate the wheat from the chaff. It takes expertise to accurately classify material as *Meaningful* versus *Irrelevant* versus *Unmitigated Rubbish*. The non-expert does not know how to weigh the relative merits of the information he or she possesses. The loudest voices or the websites with the highest rankings are given too much weight and awarded too much credibility. As a result, material that is useless or plain wrong often has too much influence on the consumer.

Experts help to cut through the noise and locate the signal. This is especially valuable to people who are faced with options that are difficult to compare. Such difficulty can come about because the choices are so similar (e.g. this socially responsible mutual fund versus that other socially responsible mutual fund), or because the choices are so dissimilar (e.g. whether to use monies to launch a new business venture or to enter retirement). The more emotionally impactful the decisions, the more the expert's value lies in reducing the volume of information and its associated complexity.

To take action

'Keep your options open' is a piece of advice we frequently give to teenagers as they consider which courses to take or which opportunities to pursue. It bespeaks our belief that *more options = greater happiness.*

People like options, it's true, but they frequently freeze up or bow out when faced with too many of them. One of the cleverest illustrations of that tendency comes from a now-famous supermarket study conducted by psychologists Sheena Iyengar and Mark Lepper in 2000.[5] Grocery store shoppers came upon a display that contained at different times either 6 or 24 different varieties of jams that they could sample. More variety led to a greater volume of jam *sampling*, but when the researchers looked at which display led to the greatest volume of jam *sales*, they found it was the one that offered less choice. The difference, in fact, was startling. Only 3% of customers bought jam after being exposed to 24 options, whereas 30% of visitors to the 6-variety display made a purchase.

The authors attributed the difference to a kind of decisional paralysis that set in as a result of having too many possibilities to sift through. The study spawned dozens of additional ones that sought to explore the conditions under which *more options = less action*. It has come to inform the field of consumer psychology and has led to changes in merchandising displays. Similar findings have been found in other aspects of human behaviour. For example, lonely hearts are more likely to go on dates when given an array of eight potential partners to select from than when they are shown an array of 20. Whether we're choosing sweet toppings or sweethearts, it seems we act more decisively when the options are constrained.

A similar phenomenon exists in the world of personal finance, where people often need help to move from mere contemplation into action.[6] You may be familiar with the 'snowball' method of debt repayment (made famous by radio host Dave Ramsey) or the 'envelope' method of keeping household expenses in check (made famous by your grandma). One of the reasons for the popularity of such basic approaches to financial management is that they reduce complexity and get people into action quickly. For folks who have been frozen by indecision or overwhelmed at the prospect of where to begin, these simple guidelines offer a quick, safe way to get moving in the direction of financial well-being. 'Getting going' leads to considerable spin-off effects in confidence and optimism, and increases the likelihood of similarly desirable behaviour changes in the future.

To save time

You could easily call up a YouTube video and learn all about chicken husbandry; even so, I'll bet you would prefer to buy a tray of chicken wings over raising poultry in your back yard. And notwithstanding the fact that you could readily find a manual for your particular model of car, I suspect you would rather pay a mechanic to swap out your transmission than be stuck underneath the car for days on end. Most of us will gratefully pay for help that saves us time.

Expert financial advice saves time for people who are too busy, too unskilled, too stymied, or too uninterested to do things for themselves. The timesaving frequently far exceeds just the obvious, up-front benefit. For example, by taking his business taxes to an accountant, it is evident that Fred (a self-employed musician) saves himself an initial eight or ten hours of poring over instructions and filling out forms. What is less evident are the other ways in which Fred has saved time, e.g. by not having to buy his wife flowers to make up for his grumpiness, by not having to meet with personnel from the federal taxation bureau to explain all the errors he undoubtedly would have made, etc. Some of the most important time savings are the ones your clients may never even be aware that you've given them. When developing marketing materials, be sure to include the time-saving benefits of your services.

To offload unpleasantness

This reason is closely related to the previous point. Having access to expertise goes beyond cost–benefit analyses involving the relative value of our time versus someone else's. Access to expertise reduces both stress and drudgery. It's not just that I would find transmission-swapping and chicken-wrangling to be time-consuming – I would also find them to be difficult, dirty and downright *yucky* tasks.

In 1993, lifestyle pioneers Joe Dominguez and Vicki Robin published a book that would become one of the iconic, counter-cultural financial advice books of the last century. In *Your Money or Your Life*, they wrote about the exchange that people make to earn a living: namely, life energy (predominantly in the form of time and talent) in exchange for money. They challenged readers to think more deeply about that transaction, ensuring that the exchange of time for money was truly worth it to them.

Since that book was first published, there has been much scholarly research done to try and elucidate the connection between money and life satisfaction. The findings are clear that there *is* a positive correlation between the two. The offloading of unpleasant activities contributes significantly to that correlation. Having disposable income allows people to hire others to do those things they'd rather not do themselves. And since 'Dealing with finances' is right up there with 'Having a root canal' and 'Waxing the bikini line' on the list of Things Most People Find Unpleasant, financial experts have something of considerable value to offer to a great many people. (Sigh. If only it were possible to offload root canals and hair removal, too.)

To make someone else happy

Some clients show up in your office solely for the purpose of making someone else happy … or to get someone else off their back. (In my clinical practice, I refer to this as the Parole Officer Model of service delivery.) If you have been in the business for a while, you, too, undoubtedly have had people in your office who are there at someone else's behest. They may be there to set up a prenuptial agreement, or because they have come into a trust fund, or because they are facing bankruptcy proceedings. They may be the spouses of longtime clients, those silent partners whose names are on all your paperwork but who never darken your door unless forced to do so. They may be overnight millionaires who just made it big in business or won a lottery, and who have been counselled to 'talk to someone' about how to deal with their changed circumstances.

Whatever the precipitating factor, such clients are often sent to you during times of tumult and change in their personal lives. Although this may not seem like an ideal situation, your help can result in remarkable peace of mind for the individual and his or her family or wider social network. It can take a little extra time and sensitivity from you to get past their initial resentment, embarrassment or discomfort over having been sent to you, but it is possible to form a vibrant working relationship with such folks.

Odds are high that they truly do need some help. It's equally likely that the people who sent them to you need some help, too. Your task is to figure out whether it's *your* help that is needed first and foremost (as opposed to the help of a therapist, attorney, or bond bailsman), and, if so, how to increase the likelihood that they will make use of it. We will be examining ways to do so in Chapters 6 and 7.

To increase confidence

Another common reason for consulting with experts is to increase confidence about an intended plan of action. Individuals want to make sure they have not overlooked any important considerations that could end up disadvantaging them. You bring extra value to the advising relationship when you employ different decision-making strategies or consult different sources of information than the clients would use on their own.

A study undertaken by the Financial Planning Standards Council of Canada has confirmed the value of the profession in this regard.[7] The study followed Canadians whose net worth spanned the gamut from modest to wealthy.[8] The results revealed significant increases in the financial and emotional well-being of clients who had consulted comprehensively with financial planners. Quite strikingly, there were marked increases in confidence apparent in every domain surveyed. Not only did expert financial advice increase people's confidence that they were on track to meet important future goals, but it also increased their confidence they could deal with setbacks in life without having to forego some of the good things that money can buy in the here-and-now. Similar increases in confidence were highlighted by the Fidelity Retirement 20/20 survey report in 2017.[9]

Many financial advisors can cite examples of grievous *over*-confidence in people from their own client list.* While such clients stick out in our memory, they are not typical. It is much more common for people to seek advice because they are unsure of something, and are concerned that what they don't know could hurt them. They want to leave your office with the certainty they have considered all of the pertinent factors and

---

* Humans are drawn to seek the opinions of people who are just like them, and are more than twice as likely to favour evidence that confirms their own thinking. This phenomenon has been labelled *confirmation bias*, and is something to be watchful for both in oneself and in one's clients. When faced with a client who is 'prickly' or highly opinionated, advisors may grow reluctant to bring contradictory information to his or her attention, preferring instead to acquiesce or soft-pedal the differences in opinion.

have settled on a satisfactory plan of action. If you can provide them with that confidence, they are more likely to persist with what they need to do.

To help make better tradeoffs

Consider the following questions:

> Is it best to choose the lower monthly pension amount and ensure a greater survivor benefit, or opt for higher monthly payments from the outset?

> Am I better off by moving to a bigger, less expensive house in the suburbs where I'd have to commute longer distances, or by staying in my tiny city house where everything is close by?

> Should I leave my fortune to my ingrate grandkids, or give it all to the Squirrel Rescue Sanctuary?

These are questions that can't be answered with factual information alone. Crunching the numbers can give some guidance, but that's only the beginning. What really improves the quality of decision-making is personalized attention from someone who knows your family history, your lifestyle preferences, and your values – or, at least, someone who is willing to take the time to have those kinds of conversations with you.

Dan Ariely is a psychology professor and the author of several bestselling books on behavioural economics. He has devoted his career to the study of how and why people make the decisions they do. One of his most robust core findings is that people often *do not know how to choose rationally*, let alone wisely. Fortunately, he assures us, people can be helped to make better tradeoffs just by being asked to consider some of the things they normally overlook or are prone to overvalue. In light of this need, he asserts that financial advisors should radically rethink what they have to offer their clients. Instead of spending an hour fine-tuning a client's investment portfolio in advance of an annual meeting, argues Ariely, an advisor would offer greater benefit talking with the client about spending and savings patterns and the tradeoffs involved in day-to-day decisions.

Ariely has found that advisors presented with this proposal usually argue strenuously against it.[10] 'That's not my job!' they protest. 'Why not?' Ariely pushes back. Who else is equipped to help someone with decisions involving both actuarial and lifestyle considerations? Doing so blends both the technical and the personal sides of advising at the highest levels.

To receive encouragement

My congregation was recently asked to fill out a survey regarding why people attend weekly church services. One of the main questions was, 'What do you most want to experience as a result of coming to church?'

Top answer: Encouragement.

Heck, yeah!

I see the same yearning in my financial therapy practice on a daily basis. People who come to see me usually have some kind of painful money history or current dilemma. They may have made bad investment decisions or overspent. They may have been exploited or experienced a huge hit to their lifestyle due to a major personal setback such as job loss or divorce. Because of the secrecy and shame that attend financial matters for many people, they may find themselves to be short on support and encouragement when they need those things the most.

Warmth and good cheer are rarely misplaced, but they are especially vital to clients who are trying to change longstanding habits. When the behaviour change is daunting, long-lasting, preventative, or unusual for their social circle, your encouragement can go a long way to helping people persist. Too often, however, financial change agents cut clients loose once they've demonstrated just two or three months of positive behaviour change. That is just around the time that clients' enthusiasm starts to flag, or they get hit with an unexpected life event, or their deadbeat cousin shows up and starts pressuring them to do something contrary to the plan you've co-created.

To have someone to blame

One of the blessings of disposable income in my life is that it allows me to hire a housecleaner. Having such a person come into our home offers some of the benefits cited in the previous pages – 'time savings' and 'offloading of unpleasant tasks' chief among them. But one unexpected benefit of a housecleaner has been that *there's always someone for me to blame when something goes missing!* (Just to be clear: I blame her only in my head, not out loud. Because it never actually *is* her fault. It's really the kids'. Or the dog's.)

Evidently, I'm not alone in finding it comforting to have someone to blame. I have had many couples report to me that they hired a financial expert because they did not want to deal with the other's wrath if something went wrong in their family business or retirement planning. There is some research support for this notion. In a 2016 study, researchers confirmed that some people 'delegate primarily to cede responsibility and blame' rather than for the more logical reason of benefitting from wise counsel.[11] Just imagine the marketing fun you could have with that one!

To feel safer

Seen from a different perspective, *having someone else to* blame *if things go wrong* could be construed as a darkly funny variant of *trusting in someone's expertise to keep you safe*. Of course, feeling safer goes way beyond the blame phenomenon. People consult with experts because they want to experience that calm, settled state that I highlighted at the beginning of this chapter.

In his book *Pre-Suasion: A Revolutionary Way to Influence and Persuade*, social psychologist Robert Cialdini discusses the influential effects of experts on decision-making. When people are unsure of what to do or how to think, the existence of someone with presumed legitimacy or expertise seems to invite people to behave like cyclists on the Tour de France: They tuck in and draft behind someone they trust.

Functional neuroimaging studies allow scientists to see what happens to brain activity as people are put through a variety of cognitive tasks. Evidence shows that the presence of an expert can change the very way our brains process information – or, indeed, cease to process information. In one study[12] that journalist Jason Zweig has dubbed 'Your Brain on Investment Advice', participants were tasked with making difficult financial decisions either on their own or with some input from an identified expert. When left unassisted to decide on the relative merits of a given option, subjects showed increased activity in the areas of the brain involved in weighing options and opinions. That was an entirely unremarkable finding. That's what was expected of brains working hard to reach a decision. But that all changed when subjects were offered access to the advice of someone identified as an expert economist. Under that condition, structures involved in active decision-making seemed to go into hibernation. The brains of people under conditions of expert economic advice looked a lot like the brains of people at prayer: trusting; non-critical; safe.

These findings should make you blanch, at least a little. Clients put a lot of faith in your presumed expertise. While that is generally a good thing, it can be a dangerous thing, too. This goes well beyond the obvious *Don't be a Bernie Madoff* injunction. The 'tuck and draft' model can offer a convenient excuse for continued ignorance among financially avoidant clients who want to remain that way. It has fiduciary implications for you, the advisor: How do you get truly informed consent from clients who trust you implicitly and who would happily sign any piece of paper you give to them, regardless of whether they understand its contents? Advice-giving under such circumstances requires advisors to be extra-scrupulous about understanding their client's hopes and concerns, surpassing the rather perfunctory and unhelpful 'Know Your Client' protocols required by many companies. Doing your due diligence in this regard serves to enhance safety at all levels, for both you and the client.

What gets in the way of these aims?

The preceding pages summarize the chief aims behind asking for advice and the most powerful advantages of receiving it. Sometimes, of course, people may not know what their true motivation is for reaching out. They may say that they want expert input when what they really want is external confirmation. They may say that they're looking for more information when what they really crave is more discernment. There can be a further disconnect between what the client is asking for and what the advisor is attempting to address. Such discrepancies or mismatches can contribute to good advice being ignored.

A further problem with respect to advice-seeking involves the advice-giver moving too quickly into offering solutions. A justifiable confidence in their capability can lead seasoned and rookie professionals alike to launch prematurely into offering solutions, before they've fully ascertained the client's reasons for reaching out. This is a major turn-off, and a chief contributor to non-adherence.

A related problem is the tendency of some professionals to dominate the discussion, especially during that all-important first meeting. Out of a desire to impress or instill confidence or seal the deal, financial professionals talk about their 'process', their superiority over their competitors, their array of offerings … you get the picture. But clients rarely give a rat's patootie about our process. They just want to know they're in good hands with us. And the best way for that to happen is for us to spend time finding out why they've come to see us.

If you want to create engaged, satisfied clients, it is crucial that you signal your willingness to meet their needs right from the outset of your involvement. You do this by determining what the client (or potential client) wants to experience or achieve as a result of meeting with you. It is vital that you ask what that desired experience or goal is, every time you meet, even if you're pretty certain you already know the answer. Here's why asking is important:

It's courteous.

It encourages efficient use of meeting time. (Remember that these questions were initially developed for health care practitioners. If neurosurgeons are convinced of the ultimate time savings these kinds of questions confer, you, too, can trust that they will offer efficiencies for you.)

It zeroes in on the issues of primary concern to the client, thus signalling your commitment to being a Thinking Partner.

It facilitates the emergence of concerns that clients might otherwise be reluctant to bring forward.

When working with couples, it helps ensure you meet the needs of both parties.

Summary

The fundamental reason that people seek advice in any domain of life is because they want help in solving a problem. They are experiencing some level of uncertainty or reluctance at the prospect of dealing with the problem on their own. Even when a given problem seems entirely cerebral or purely factual in terms of its content and/or its solution, there is always an emotional aspect to advice-seeking. That's because uncertainty causes a certain degree of discomfort or suffering, ranging from the miniscule to the alarming. When that cognitive uncertainty is resolved, that internal tension is eased and emotional settling occurs.

People seek advice to solve a problem, so that they can feel more settled as a result. The more you can contribute to this settling, the more trusted and valuable an advisor you will be to them.

Adherence Boosters

1. Make a point of establishing a clear agenda at the outset of every meeting. Ask:

    > What would make our time together today the best use of your time, energy and money?

    > What are you hoping will happen as a result of our meeting?

2. Sometimes the answers will seem self-evident by virtue of the service you provide. A tax preparer, for example, can be

reasonably sure that most clients would just like their taxes done. If this is the case for you, then modify the questions as you see fit, but do make a point both of determining the objectives and of ensuring you have met them. For example:

> Aside from the obvious, is there anything else that brings you here today?

3. It is sometimes possible to establish an agenda ahead of time, by e-mail, with returning clients. Be sure that you re-confirm the agenda at the start of the meeting, as additional concerns may have arisen. Make sure that you return to the agenda when you still have five or ten minutes left in your time together. Ask the following:

> When I asked you about what you most wanted to accomplish as a result of our meeting today, you told me (insert answer here). Did we accomplish that?

> What else would you like us to cover before we wrap up?

4. Finally, make sure that nothing happened to cause the opposite of what you were hoping to achieve.

> Is there anything that is leaving you unsettled or unsure?

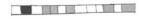

Now it's time to turn to the FACTS, and do a more in-depth examination of those five factors that contribute to follow-through with your advice. I'm going to start with the 'T' factor

– you and your team – as this sets the stage for how you view your opportunities and responsibilities with respect to all of the other domains.*

---

* Astute readers will have noticed that this decision effectively turns the acronym FACTS into TFACS. Many of you will undoubtedly be twitching, as a result. Please accept my apologies, take a deep breath, and move on. It's good for your brain to be non-linear, on occasion.

Chapter 3

A Curse, a Plague, and Other Problems Caused by Advisory Teams

WARNING: THIS CHAPTER MAY BE INSULTING TO SOME READERS

Disclaimer: It's not my fault. It's just the FACTS.

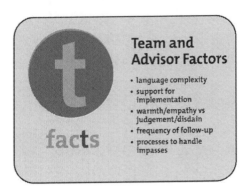

Team and Advisor Factors
- language complexity
- support for implementation
- warmth/empathy vs judgement/disdain
- frequency of follow-up
- processes to handle impasses

According to research findings, one of the major contributors to non-adherence is *you* – you, the advisor, along with the team that surrounds and supports you in your work with clients. All too often, practitioners make mistakes that predictably lead to confusion, unreturned forms, emotional upset, doomed homework assignments, ignored messages, impulsive investment decisions, and outright termination of the client-advisor relationship.

It's easy to grow impatient with clients at such moments of impasse, and to exclaim, 'I did not sign up for this! I have a proven track record of giving solid advice. People can just take it or leave it.' But that would be a big mistake, one that is increasingly less tolerated in many other spheres of life. From industry to government to health care, the *supplier side* of products and information is under pressure to ensure that it is easier for end users to do the right thing than the wrong thing: 'Make a tamper-proof safety switch for this machine.' 'Figure out the most effective signage for this ski hill.' 'Make this pill bottle harder for kids to open but easier for seniors to get into.' Financial professionals need to catch up with the rest of the world and accept the fact that they play a critical role in ensuring that their advice gets implemented.

Are there clients that you should not work with? Absolutely! Serial non-adherence can be a tip-off that a given client is not someone that you should keep in your book of business, both for ethical reasons and for your own well-being. (This is dealt with at greater length in Chapter 10.) But before you throw someone overboard, give some serious thought to whether you are making some of the cardinal errors that are known to sink the advising relationship.

ADVISOR AND TEAM MISTAKE #1:
Not seeing adherence as a shared responsibility

The most effective advisors will always be the ones who understand that they are responsible for giving advice that is customized to the client, timely, and as easy to implement as possible. They actively seek ways to ensure follow-through – both their own and their clients'. In turn, they make it known that they expect certain things from the client, things that they let the client know about in advance. Such practitioners have a 'growth mindset' with respect to the shared responsibility for adherence, enlisting their entire team to look for ways of ensuring that all tasks get done by all parties.

From confident to cocky and clueless

When it comes to valuing their technical knowledge and recommendations, smart service providers can develop a level of confidence that tips over into arrogance or cockiness. Their self-assurance of their expertise, combined with their desire to be efficient and effective, can result in a top-down approach to their craft that is out of step with both the science of adherence and truly excellent advising. Here are some of the fundamental beliefs that, however well-intended, can lead to arrogance in service delivery:

> We are the experts, here to direct you. We will act in your best interest, guiding you ethically and competently. In turn, you will tell us everything we need to know, and either do the things we recommend or allow us to do them for you. If you do not heed our advice, you are being wrong-headed. At such times, we will increase the persuasiveness of our arguments to get you to comply. If we cannot, we will wash our hands of you.

What's the problem with this approach, you may well ask. You may know of some very successful people and firms who seem to operate on this basis.* The first problem is that it is based on a number of false premises. Chief among them is the notion that it is even *possible* to provide quality advice without devoting time to uncovering client experiences, beliefs, expectations and knowledge that may differ materially from yours. Such differences are not always incidental, inconvenient or irrelevant. They may be entirely germane to what clients need from you – and to what you need to receive from them in order to give recommendations that truly meet the ethical standards of your profession. It is not good practice to resist knowing their take on things.

Another mistaken assumption is that all clients are capable of full disclosure and cooperation at all times. Elsewhere in this book, I discuss how such things as painful money histories, associated trust issues, and major life changes can put a stick in the spokes of progress. They can wreak havoc on the intellectual and energy resources clients need to implement your recommendations.

A further false premise is that clients who disagree with you are, by definition, *just plain wrong*. Time for an ego check. You may be good, but you are not infallible! Subtly and unfortunately, clients of arrogant advisory teams learn to stifle their expressions of uncertainty or disagreement. This top-down approach is based on a hierarchical and old-fashioned model of advising that tends not to go over well with younger clients,

---

* Such an approach tends to work well, at least initially, with clients who are culturally similar to you, very busy, and/or high on trust.

who have been raised with the belief that their opinions and input matter.

Finally, this approach offers little in the way of value-added service provision, particularly in the relational domain, and thus leaves you vulnerable to losing clients to cheaper competitors. It makes you a sitting duck for being fired by clients in the aftermath of major life transitions that have challenged their fundamental sense of self. Many a 'perfect' long-time client abruptly ends the advising relationship at such a juncture, as they do not have the confidence that you will take the time to understand their new reality. Indeed, 'failure to understand clients' goals and objectives' has been identified as one of the top five reasons advisors are fired, second only to 'failure to communicate on a timely basis.'[13] Such clients often rightly conclude that the advisor is clueless as to what they need and want from the relationship.

When empathy becomes a problem

If the arrogant advisor can be accused of being *too hard* with respect to adherence demands on the client, an excessively empathic advisor can be accused of being *too soft*. As heretical as it might seem to some readers, there is such a thing as being too attuned to the client's emotional state.

In his 2016 book, *Against Empathy: The Case for Rational Compassion*, psychologist Paul Bloom argues that it is entirely possible to take empathy too far. Among the problems associated with excessive empathy are a spreading of emotional distress that leaves observers less capable of offering help than they would otherwise be; a tendency to lose sight of the bigger picture; and knee-jerk responses to stop the pain as quickly as possible.

I have witnessed this dynamic at work in some of the financial professionals I coach. For example, I have seen trustees who drag their feet at initiating discussions on pre-nuptial agreements, as they don't want to cast the gloomy rain cloud over someone's happy parade. I have worked with planners who pull their punches in addressing calamitous overspending because they fear causing upset or adding to family conflict. I repeatedly hear from advisors who find it difficult to provide any push-back whatsoever to clients' panic-driven demands to 'Sell everything!' or excited insistence to 'Buy now!' By being too responsive to their client's emotional state, such professionals fail to serve their clients' long-term interests. The solid ground offered by the professionals' technical competency and training gets exchanged for the quicksand of excessive personal attunement. Nobody benefits by this exchange.

The wrong kind of attunement can even contribute to ethical violations. It is a risk that has been flagged for psychologists, for whom empathy (along with a good box of tissues) has long been viewed as a fundamental tool of the trade. One study found that a third of therapists felt they would be unable to bring themselves to do the right thing if faced, for example, with having to address a colleague's unethical behaviour. They would simply find the emotions involved to be too uncomfortable to handle.[14] It's as though there are two kinds of ethics at war in us: the more abstract, higher-order considerations outlined in our ethical codes, versus the stickier, here-and-now imperative to not cause distress to anyone (including ourselves). Knowing the ethically right thing to do does not equip us emotionally to do it.[15] Too much empathy can get in the way of intelligent and right action.

The 'just right' advisor

Like Goldilocks, we need to find that *just right* ground, which in our case means the right ground between being an arrogant hardass and a squishy marshmallow. That is best achieved by keeping Mistake #1 in mind, and remembering to view adherence as a shared responsibility. In a talk she delivered to the Financial Planning Association in 2012, *Willful Blindness* author Margaret Heffernan made it clear that she approves of the notion of Thinking Partners when it comes to the advisor–client relationship. The key requirement, she elucidated, is that both parties have to be intentional about ceding a little of their authority or autonomy to the other. The financial professional doesn't know everything that he or she needs to know about the client; the client doesn't know everything that he or she needs to know about money. With this acknowledgement, both parties are freer to explore, question assumptions, and ask what might actually be wrong with a plan instead of the more normal tendency to look for confirmatory evidence.[16]

When you're so good, people become suspicious …

Here's what shared adherence looks like when it's done well.

In the building where I work, a number of my medical colleagues conduct medication research trials for hard-to-treat auto-immune diseases. They must comply with scientifically rigorous protocols throughout the study period, tracking many aspects of patients' disease indicators as well as a number of adherence variables: missed appointments, skipped dosages, dropout rates, etc. Some time ago, one of the pharmaceutical companies ordered an immediate halt to a study, and commenced an emergency audit. The problem? Excessively high adherence rates were being reported by my colleagues. Auditors were dispatched from drug company headquarters to find out what was skewing the data. Did the researchers not understand how to code absences or missed dosages? Were they deliberately disguising their results in an attempt to look better? What was going on?!

I could have told them to save the trip. My colleagues were not committing scientific fraud. Rather, they had pulled out all the stops to make it as easy as possible for patients to do what they were supposed to do. More strikingly, the staff did it with such a high degree of emotional warmth and connectedness that patients looked forward to coming into the office. The patients cited the helpfulness of the research coordinator in arranging transportation, the welcoming kindness of the receptionists every time they walked in, the attentiveness with which the doctors listened to their updates. Every day, those research subjects carried out tasks that were unpleasant (injecting themselves with experimental medications) and time-consuming (filling out paperwork). The patients kept their commitments with a consistency unseen in other research sites. They reported to the astonished auditors that they would feel bad if they didn't carry out the instructions, as it would be letting the doctors and staff down. One of the auditors joked with me afterwards, 'I almost wish I had a disease so that I could be a research subject at this clinic!'

Meanwhile, just down the hall, was little ol' me. How, I wondered, would the adherence rates seen in my solo practice stack up if I were ever to undergo a surprise audit? Were they anywhere close to those achieved by my colleagues? I was chagrinned to admit that, no, they weren't. I figured I could cut myself some slack for not having drug company resources behind me to help create such an excellent support team. But when my subsequent attempts to get corporate sponsorship from both Cadbury and Victoria's Secret failed miserably, I knew I would have to find some low-cost ways to improve my adherence rates. I went back to the literature to figure out what changes would pack the biggest wallop. The result of that adherence exploration made a huge difference for me and my clients ... and led to the writing of this book. When you begin to implement the recommendations outlined in this and other chapters, you, too, will soon be suspicion-worthy in all the right ways!

Let's consider three additional mistakes that advisors and teams need to avoid.

ADVISOR AND TEAM MISTAKE #2:
Making people feel stupid

You know all those times when you've fretted over what you would do with your couch in the event of a heavy rain? No? Well, me neither, but apparently at least two people have. One of those two invented an inflatable raft that is placed underneath furniture, ready at a moment's notice to be pumped up in the event of flood waters in the living room. The second of the two was an inexperienced but wealthy investor who decided to pour $70,000 into (pardon the pun) *launching* the invention.

The notion of inflatable furniture rafts may be supremely goofy, but it *is* easy to visualize and understand. And it's that easy-to-comprehend factor that all clients want their advisors to offer to them when discussing the complex world of personal and business finance. That's what results in the crucial emotional and cognitive *settling* (discussed in Chapter 3) for which people seek you out in the first place.

Making complex ideas easily understood takes a special kind of genius. It's rare to see it done well. Consider what baseball star Torii Hunter told *Sports Illustrated* contributor Pablo Torre about his experience of speaking to reputable financial professionals: 'Once you get into the financial stuff, it sounds like Japanese.' Or the words of football player 'Rocket' Ismail: 'I once had a meeting with (a major investment firm) ... and it was literally like listening to Charlie Brown's teacher.' Ismail contrasts that with a meeting he had with a music label producer, with whom he later disastrously invested: 'The guy was a real good talker.' [17] As it turns out, so are most people who later are revealed to be con artists, and at least some of the people with supremely goofy ideas.

When being smart is a problem

How about you? Are you a 'real good talker'? Most of us are not – at least, not in the way that our clients need us to be. What they need is for us to speak *their* language. But the more educated we are, the harder that becomes.

Roberto Trotta is a professor in astrophysics, a domain that some people find a tad difficult to comprehend. Some years ago, he decided to take on a colleague's challenge to make science easier to understand for the general public. The end product of that challenge is Trotta's book, *The Edge of the Sky: All You Need to Know About All-There-Is*, which explains theories about the universe using only the most common 1,000 words in English. (Just to give you a sense of the magnitude of that challenge, Trotta could not use the words *universe, particles,* or *galaxies* in his writing.) While this labour may be seen as an unusually extreme commitment to making oneself understood, it is interesting to note what happened in the months after the book's publication: It became a bestseller, and Trotta became a sought-after speaker. People loved the experience of being able to understand astrophysics.

Neuroscientist and author Daniel Levitin describes what it feels like to work with people who are one, two, or three levels above you with respect to their knowledge base. He argues that it is easier to learn from people who are just one level above (or who, like Trotta, communicate as though they were). When two levels separate you, he explains: 'You're barely speaking the same language … You can still learn from them if you don't get discouraged … You don't think they'll help you – but for some reason, they do.' By the time somebody is three levels ahead of you, says Levitin, 'they're speaking a different language'. He claims that, paradoxically, they may seem less knowledgeable to you than the folks one or two levels below them, because 'you won't be able to even imagine what they think about, or why.'[18]

This is a problem known as the 'Curse of Knowledge'. Once we know something, we are changed by the knowing of it, and find it difficult to remember that other people don't know that thing, too. Think of all the knowledge you gathered by the end of your coursework and credentialing that you did not possess beforehand – how many of Levitin's levels did it advance you? The vocabulary changes alone are staggering. The number of new terms learned by physicians in the course of their training exceeds the 13,000 mark.[19] No corresponding study has been done regarding terminology learned by financial professionals, but I suspect the data would be similar. You have learned the specialized concepts and terminology associated with economic theories, statistics, tax codes, lending regulations, investment vehicles, insurance products, market forces … it goes on and on.

When that specialized, professional vocabulary slips into your conversations with clients, it can quickly overwhelm their capacity to keep up with you. What results is an emotional state that is the polar opposite of what you're aiming for: namely, feelings of inadequacy and insufficiency rather than confidence and calm. A 2017 study into the failure of financial education programmes takes direct aim at the emotional impact of technically complex materials prepared for the general population. Respondents told study co-author Nick Throp that many initiatives 'made them feel stupid and guilty for a lack of understanding. If they're starting from this perspective, it makes it difficult for them to engage with the overall message.'[20]

Similar stories are recounted by the participants in my 'Women and Money' groups when I ask why they do not currently have an accountant or a financial planner. Somebody, at some point, left them feeling stupid and embarrassed during a meeting, and they never again plucked up the courage to go speak to someone else. Much of this problem could be avoided if advisors would only trust that they do not need to impress or educate clients as much as they need to understand and involve them.

ADVISOR AND TEAM MISTAKE #3:
Talking too much

As if the Curse of Knowledge weren't hard enough to deal with, advisors must also overcome the 'Plague of Blather'. Too many advisors mistakenly assume that their value to a client is measured by the amount of information they provide. Once the initial pleasantries are over, many professionals launch into wordy descriptions of their background, their qualifications, their processes, their investment rationale … and so forth and so on, long past the time when the client has started to glaze over. This is often compounded by the provision of multi-page comprehensive plans that are never read, because they, too, use excessively complex language and are far too long.

Client satisfaction, it turns out, is directly related to the amount of airtime that the *client* takes up in meetings. You need to get them talking about all of the key issues identified throughout this book, and you need to cultivate the art of deep listening as they do so. That is the only way you will be able to deliver advice that is on-target both factually and emotionally for the client, leading to the kind of settled state that you want to help create for them.

My experience in coaching both health care and financial professionals is that it is damnably hard to get them to stop talking. Case in point: It takes the average physician just 18 seconds to interrupt the average patient during a typical interview.[21] Patients are able to finish their opening statements about why they are in the office less than 25% of the time before the physician barges in.[22] Once again, no comparable figures exist with respect to financial professionals' tendency to interrupt, but I'd wager that the findings would be just as bad, if not worse.

Too much to retain

You may be protesting at this point that you have highly educated clients who are completely able to comprehend everything you say. The Curse of Knowledge may truly be less of a problem when working with such clients, but the Plague of Blather is not. Research shows that highly educated clients are better at *understanding*, but fare no better than their less-learned counterparts when it comes to *remembering and following* the crucial content of recommendations. When major life stressors happen, educated clients become just as depleted as their less-educated peers, and find it just as hard to summon up the needed energy to focus, remember, and engage. If you were to liken brains to automobiles, you could say that educated clients may have higher-powered engines, but they have the same size of gas tank and the same number of seats. There are still limits to their capacity.

Too little to hold on to

It's important to make a distinction between non-adherence that is *unintentional* versus *intentional*. One of the major contributors to unintentional non-adherence is the problem of forgetting. The longer meetings last, and the longer *you* talk, the greater the likelihood that clients will forget what they agreed to do in response (and why).

In turn, one of the biggest contributors to intentional non-adherence is the client's lack of emotional connection to the plan you devise for them. Sudden Money® Institute founder Susan Bradley asserts that both engagement and adherence increase when clients are helped to get in touch with their deepest sense of purpose and meaning, and then co-create plans that are in alignment with that meaning. Such clients are invested emotionally – not just intellectually and financially – in the recommended course of action. Task completion occurs more promptly and reliably with engaged clients.

The more time you devote to listening, the easier it becomes to give clients such a positive experience. This results in escalating success in both engagement and adherence, since resonant and meaningful content is much more readily remembered and acted upon. More listening on your part also increases the likelihood that clients will come up with their own solutions for many of their problems. Again, the payoff for this is that clients are more likely to implement solutions that they, themselves, have generated.

ADVISOR AND TEAM MISTAKE #4:
Letting judgment get in the way

My son's piano teacher told me the following story:

The little boy was only four years old. When it was his turn to play that heart-rending classic, 'Mary Had a Little Lamb', he marched up to the stage with a big smile. He bowed to the audience, sat down, and executed a flawless performance – except for the wee problem that he played everything four notes higher than he ought to have.

It seems the tyke had developed the habit of finding middle C by looking for a certain letter in the piano manufacturer's name (printed in gilt letters above the keyboard). Once he found that letter, he could be confident that middle C was just below it. Unfortunately, the piano in the concert room had a different brand name, with letters that fell above entirely different notes on the keyboard. And so the resulting performance, while technically perfect, was a little off. At the end of the piece, the little guy got off the stool, bowed to the audience, and then made the indignant pronouncement, 'That is a terrible piano!'

Anyone who gives advice for a living will be tempted, at some point, to blame the piano. It's kind of cute in a four-year-old; in adults, less so. In truth, it's an unfortunate and ineffective habit to get into, but I see it (and do it, myself) all too often.

There is no way *not* to judge others. It's how we're wired, neurologically, and it has undoubtedly contributed to the survival success of our ancestors. But like any other cognitive heuristic (or mental shortcut), the judgments we make about other people are prone to error. We see a small sample of their behaviour, and jump to conclusions about how they behave the rest of the time. We hear a portion of their story, and start slotting them into broad categories of Good/Bad, Smart/Dumb, Spoiled/Deserving, Capable/Helpless. That's just about when the inevitable confirmation bias kicks in, making it harder for us to see and accept evidence that they may be something other than what we've determined they are. We are especially prone to forming negative impressions about people when their decisions and emotional responses are different from our own.

In some offices, scathing opinions and rude statements about clients are routinely allowed to fly around the room, unchallenged. It is crucial that you work to put a stop to this bad habit. It's fine for team members to acknowledge that they find certain clients annoying, or heart-tugging, or difficult to work with; such admissions can lead to the provision of support and the generation of ideas for making it easier to work with them. What is not fine are the nicknames, eye rolls, and jokes made at clients' expense. A good litmus test is this: If the clients in question were to hear the comments being made about them, would they be offended? If so, then your team's tendency to 'let 'er rip' should be reined in.

Dealing with strong emotions

You will undoubtedly be present during times of intensely positive and negative client emotion. At certain times, that emotion will be directed at you, regardless of whether you 'deserve' it. When the markets undergo a sharp decline, when a tax bill is unexpectedly high, or when people realize that their net worth has just ballooned beyond anything they ever imagined, chances are high that they will have something strong to feel – and then, something strong to say – about that. At other times, strong emotion about personal beliefs and events will simply be expressed in your presence (rather than directed at you). Virtually everyone who works with people's finances must meet with people going through life transitions that are emotionally evocative – widowhood, retirement, business sales, etc.

Ronald Duska, Ph.D., is a business ethicist who writes and consults extensively for financial services professionals. [23] He posits that financial professionals have an ethical obligation to help clients with the emotional and existential aspects of financial crises, not just the numbers aspects. That's a tall order! It assumes that you have the ability to engage clients in discussions of deep personal import. It assumes that you've done your own values clarification and exploration with respect to money. And it assumes that you know the limits of your own competence and scope of professional offerings, so that you know when it's time to make referrals to therapists and other needed allies.

In light of the inevitability of encountering emotional clients, you should hone your skills in staying present and grounded during such times. After years spent working with a wide range of financial professionals, I believe the emotional skills of *equanimity* and *warmth* are the primary ones to work on. Equanimity is that quality that allows you to remain calm and composed in the presence of strong emotion, without being defensive, callous, reactive, or undone by it. It requires considerable skill in self-management. In their must-read book, *Facilitating Financial Health,* authors Brad Klontz, Rick Kahler and Ted Klontz suggest that more financial professionals should consider doing the self-reflection that promotes such equanimity.[24] This can involve doing 'whatever is necessary to become conscious of your own money scripts' (i.e. your deeply entrenched financial beliefs and values) as well as working with a therapist or coach for the purposes of growth and/or healing.[25]

When such steadfastness is accompanied by interpersonal warmth, you are likely to be viewed by clients as someone who always has their best interests at heart. By contrast, without the warmth, you will come across like Mr. Spock from *Star Trek* or Sheldon from *The Big Bang Theory* – great 'quant' guys, perhaps, but not somebody who would shine in a client-facing role. What Spock and Sheldon and every stiff advisory team member need to work on are (1) eye contact, (2) nodding, and (3) smiling. These are the three primary behaviours associated with the quality of warmth.[26]

Dr. Edward Johnson is an expert on the factors that contribute to a positive working alliance with clients. In his book, *Working Together in Clinical Supervision,* Johnson stresses that warmth is a key component of the emotional connection that professionals must cultivate with clients. When combined with a mutual agreement on goals and tasks, that warmth is what builds a solid alliance between client and advisor. The relationship itself becomes part of what enables clients to persist on the tasks required for goal achievement, especially when the going gets tough.[27]

Summary

Advisors can contribute mightily to the problem of advice being ignored. To prevent this, you and your team need to view adherence as a responsibility you share with the client throughout the client engagement process. Advisors contribute to non-adherence when they use language and concepts that are not familiar to the clients, when they dominate meetings by talking too much, and when they take a judgment-laden, critical stance towards clients.

Adherence Boosters

Commit to implementing one or more of the following strategies:

1. Educate your team about non-adherence. Ensure that all team members understand that adherence is a responsibility they share jointly with your clients. Increase their emotional connection to this notion by asking them to share examples of non-adherence that stress, delay, or concern them. Ask them to consider the difference it could make in their work if the frequency of such problems were to decrease.

2. For a month, record every instance of non-adherence that you and your team encounter – whether it's yours, the team's, or the clients'. In a team meeting specially designated for such a purpose, brainstorm several solutions for the most common or problematic behaviours noted. You may choose to comb through the strategies in this book to see if any of them apply, or you may generate some novel solutions of your own. Decide which adherence-boosting strategy each of you will commit to employing for the next month. (Not every team member will necessarily need to work on the same thing.) Four weeks later, report back in on the effects of your interventions. Adjust accordingly, and apply for another thirty days. Do this exercise at least once a year.

3. Forgetfulness is a huge contributor to unintentional non-adherence. Combat this by making sure you have a system for implementing the strategies you want to adopt (whether from this chapter or any other ones). For example:

> Print out the agenda-setting questions from Chapter 2. Ask them at the outset of each meeting. At the end, check in to see whether they have met their goals for the meeting.

> Insert the Adherence Booster questions from Chapter 4 into your existing 'Know Your Client' protocol. Record the answers where you will see them before each client contact.

4. Combat the Curse of Knowledge by becoming a 'real good talker'. Strive to make your interviews and client materials as free of professional jargon as possible. Start by taking every piece of written information you might give to a typical client, and hand it over to four or five people – either existing clients, or people who would be similar to them in major ways. Equip them with a marker and ask them to highlight every sentence whose content they do not fully understand. Compare the results. Redo those documents in client-friendly language.

5. Aim for shorter meetings: The longer meetings last, the less likely it is that clients will be able to remember what was agreed upon, and why. Send clients a quick memo within 24 hours of meeting, summarizing what was discussed and

agreed upon. Assign dates for the completion of follow-up items for both you and the clients.

6. Do not assume clients have understood the crucial aspects of what you discussed together; rather, ensure they have understood them. The same goes for making sure that you understood what they needed you to know. Ask these questions at the end of each meeting:

    > Do you feel that I have a good understanding of your situation?

    > Do you have any more questions or information for me?

    > Can you tell me in your own words what we agreed would be the next step, and why?

7. Do a warmth audit of your team. Eye contact, nodding and smiling are three of the primary behaviours associated with the quality of warmth, so that can be a good place to start your audit. Do team members routinely convey interest and a desire to continue conversation, or do they inadvertently broadcast a lack of openness and concern? Don't forget to include yourself in the audit. Ask for candid feedback from someone you trust on whether you consistently display warmth during your exchanges. If the answer is 'no', 'rarely' or 'sometimes', get some coaching. This is a skill you can improve.

8. Consider doing exit interviews with departing clients, or hiring an external source to do that for you. One of the

most upsetting things a team has to deal with is the decision of good clients to move their business elsewhere. Most businesses do not have a mechanism for finding out why this happens, when it happens. Exit interviews are a means of learning whether relationship dynamics between them and you or your team may have contributed to their leaving. Although it can be upsetting to learn of mistakes or misunderstandings that drove the client away, it is one of the most valuable forms of feedback you can receive.

Okay – enough introspection for a while! Now let's turn to the 'F' in the FACTS model, and consider what it is about the domain of finance that can make it hard for advice to stick.

Chapter 4

The Peculiarities of People and Finances

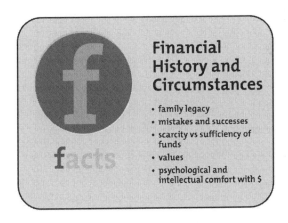

Financial History and Circumstances

- family legacy
- mistakes and successes
- scarcity vs sufficiency of funds
- values
- psychological and intellectual comfort with $

*f*acts

A tale of two heartbreaks

Two long-ago encounters started me on the path to this book. I suspect the psychology of the two characters involved, the Agitated Professor and the Wounded Lumberjack, will be familiar to you.

The Agitated Professor

I was sitting in a hospital lecture hall with a group of medical students, listening to a lesson on neuroanatomy. The class came to an abrupt halt when an agitated older professor burst onto the stage. With the briefest of apologies to his colleague for the disruption, he launched into his story. He was 68 years old, he told us. He had been a physician for nearly 40 years, earning the kind of money that most people would think was 'fabulous'. (Now he had our full attention. Most of us were still eating ramen noodles four times a week and dreaming of getting past the poverty line.) Raking his hands through his hair, he shared with us that, just minutes earlier, he had been informed by his bank that he was in no shape to retire – that he was, in fact, close to broke. He had sunk everything into a private investment 'opportunity' that turned out to be a scam.

'I've been an idiot!' he railed. 'I thought I was smarter than them all! I took crazy risks. I invested in every tax shelter going over the years, and ignored all the fundamentals of prudent investing. And now I have to go home and explain to my wife why I can't make good on my promises to her.' He was pacing like a zoo animal by this point, stopping only when he had gathered his wits enough to give us his anguished advice. 'So take a lesson from me: Don't be an idiot with your money. Get good advice. Then follow it!' And with that he exited the stage, leaving us all dumbstruck.

Fast forward a few years. I was working as a neuro-psychologist at that same university hospital when the second encounter took place:

The Wounded Lumberjack

I had a patient I'll call Jacques. He had spent the past 15 years – fully half of his life up to that point – working in the boreal forests of Manitoba. He was injured when a falling tree went 'rogue', striking him on the side of his head and shoulder. The tree took out his right eye, deafened his right ear, and crushed the nerves to his right arm. Jacques was never going to pick up a chainsaw again.

The accident put everything in jeopardy. With no disability insurance and little in the way of worker's compensation benefits, his cash flow came to an abrupt halt. His wife began a frenetic scramble to keep household finances afloat, but as the months wore on and the savings were used up and the bank and creditors lost patience, the stresses began to mount. I knew things were grave. I referred Jacques for credit counselling and to various social services agencies that could help stabilize the family's finances, but he did not follow through with any of their recommendations.

So you can imagine my bafflement when Jacques arrived for a session just a few days before Christmas, and began rattling off all the things he had bought for his family: the latest video gaming system, new hockey skates, designer clothes, a gold necklace for his wife. 'What the heck, Jacques?! Did you win the lottery? Last I heard, you guys had just managed to put together the Hydro and mortgage payments for December.' And with a solemnity I will never forget, he answered, 'I used that money for the Christmas gifts. I will *not* allow my kids to suffer because of what happened to me.'

Jacques' story did not end well. In the months after the lollapalooza Christmas, the family lost their home. The couple separated. Jacques dropped out of therapy, and for good reason: I had not been helpful in addressing the major stressor in his life.

The Agitated Professor and the Wounded Lumberjack were two men with two very different educational and vocational paths, at two very different life stages. But they suffered the same unwillingness to adopt sound financial practices, and the same disastrous consequences: dreams shattered, promises broken, families under unbearable strain.

Money and resilience

Those incidents left a deep impression on me. As I continued to work with people whose lives had been turned upside down as a result of an accident or illness, I made a point of asking more questions about their financial lives. And I learned that money mattered – but not in the way I had predicted. It wasn't income or net worth alone that determined their recovery trajectory. It was all about the financial habits and skills the patients had cultivated long before the setbacks occurred.

If, before they had an accident or fell ill, they'd been able to have frank and calm money conversations with their families, that ability was called on to good effect post-accident. If they had cultivated the habit of living below their means, that habit allowed them to minimize the creation of new debt when illness struck. If they had a financial plan in place that included insurance and savings for times of emergency, that plan carried them through the hard times.

Resilient recovery from adverse life events did not depend as much as I thought it would on the patients' socioeconomic status or earnings. Instead, resilient recovery had more to do with their pre-existing relationships to, and around, money.

Years later, my initial observations in this regard were fleshed out by findings from one of the largest global surveys ever undertaken: the Gallup study that formed the basis for the 2010 book, *Wellbeing*.[28] That study identified financial well-being as one of five key components of overall well-being, but it, too, reported that the relationship between money and health was more nuanced than one might think. A *lack of worry about money*, for example, has more than double the impact of income on overall well-being. *Financial security* – the perception that one has more than enough money to accomplish one's aims – was found to have three times the impact on well-being as does income alone.

Money and stress

For many years, the American Psychological Association has conducted wide-scale surveys, asking the general population about their leading sources of stress. And every year, the answer comes back the same: *Money* tops the list, beating out other top contenders such as work or health.[29]

In addition to being a significant concern all on its own, money is intricately interwoven into many of the other stressful domains cited by respondents: unsafe housing, inadequate health care, relationship problems. Money stress can interact with these other stressors, exacerbating them. For example, marital fights about money are associated with nastier fighting techniques and poorer relationship outcomes.[30] Similarly, workplace stress can be heightened when workers feel that there are no economically viable alternatives to their current, unhappy job.

While there are limits to what money can do for us, the things it *can* do matter profoundly to both personal and societal well-being – more profoundly, in fact, than any other secular force on the planet, according to financial planning thought leader Richard Wagner. [31] He rightly asserts that money management skills have become key to the survival of modern woman and man. Little wonder, then, that money has come to occupy such a prominent space in our psyches, and is so capable of triggering intense emotions.

What they don't teach in school

Given the connections between money, stress, and well-being in the general populace, you might think that medical schools and psychology graduate programmes would address the issue at some length. This is not the case – far from it. In the eleven years of my undergraduate, graduate, and postdoctoral studies, I had precisely two lectures that touched on money. One pointed out that patients in manic phases of a bipolar illness often spend recklessly; the other indicated that poverty is a major determinant of ill health and, therefore, ought to be avoided. Neither lecture addressed what to actually *do* for people with financial challenges. As a result, I received wondrously sound training on how to help people deal with any number of specific fears and stressors – parenting, health, spiders, work, driving – but never anything that was targeted to the main source of stress in people's lives. Like other health care professionals, I was left to 'wing it' when it came to the financial side of the human experience.

Traditional training programmes in the financial professions have fared no better at equipping their trainees to address the emotional or behavioural side of money. Certified Financial Planner (CFP®) credentialing programmes have finally started to include courses in basic interviewing and communication skills, but these courses do not include lectures specific to the challenges of communicating about money. As for targeted training in non-adherence, or the requirement that students understand their own emotions and beliefs about money? Such things are not even on the radar. As a result, financial professionals are left to 'wing it' when dealing with the human side of the financial experience.

Icebergs ahead!

Psychiatrist David Krueger postulates that our relationship with money is the longest-standing relationship we will ever have[32]. We began to be affected by money before we were even born, by virtue of such things as our mother's nutritional status and her access to health care. And, at the end, money will affect the quality of the coffin in which we are laid to rest, and the bounty of the food and drink served at our wake. Money is interlaced with every aspect of our lives, largely determining such things as where we live, how well we are educated, whom we marry, and where we work.

Many of the most significant lessons we learned about money were *absorbed* rather than *taught*. Moreover, the most vivid teachings occurred during times of heightened emotions, searing them into our psyche and wrapping them in the mantle of 'Truths That Must Not Be Questioned'. Many were learned at developmental stages when we did not have the language or the insight to fully process them. As a result, the bulk of our beliefs about money lie well below the surface of our conscious awareness. They lie there, largely undetected, until the good ships Graduation, or Marriage, or Windfall, or Setback, come along and ram right into them.

Money scripts

In *Facilitating Financial Health,* authors Klontz, Kahler and Klontz apply the term 'money scripts' to those internalized assumptions or rules about money that so frequently operate outside of conscious awareness. Here are some of the more common ones:

> I must not spend money on things I can do without.
>
> Money will take care of itself.
>
> Money should not be discussed.
>
> My parents / partner will always take care of my financial needs.
>
> Success means never lowering your income or standard of living.
>
> Money brings problems.
>
> I'm a financial screw-up.
>
> If people need something from me, it is selfish and mean to withhold it.

More money equals more happiness and security.

I must always 'look the part'.

Our family has a special responsibility to the world.

The problem with money scripts is not that they are inherently wrong, or bad, or misguided; the problem is that they are rigid and indiscriminately applied. The scripts offer no give, no suppleness. They don't gracefully get out of the way in response to changes in circumstance or major life transitions. Since financial professionals are usually called upon to work with people during times of significant life change, they will inevitably run up against those rigid underlying beliefs. You should suspect a money script violation when you encounter uncharacteristic resistance, rigidity or emotional volatility in a client you've otherwise found to be quite flexible and even-keeled.

Money and mental health

In some people, problematic beliefs and behaviours surrounding money do more than just lie quietly under the surface, causing the occasional disturbance. Rather, they come to dominate individuals' lives, causing great harm in the process. Authors Klontz, Kahler and Klontz apply the term 'money disorders' when describing 'the behavioral manifestations of damaging and disabling money scripts' (p. 93, *Facilitating Financial Health*). You need only re-scan the cases of the Agitated Professor and the Wounded Lumberjack to detect many of the signs of full-blown money disorders: strained relationships, high levels of emotional distress, health complications, profound alterations in self-identity.

There is no separate classification or category for money disorders in the DSM-5, the diagnostic manual for mental disorders; there is, however, a recognition that mental health problems can manifest through troubling financial behaviours. The previously mentioned reckless spending of manic patients is one such example. Other mental health problems with overt financial manifestations and painful consequences include pathological gambling, dependent personality disorder, an array of alcohol and drug addictions, compulsive buying, hoarding, and antisocial personality disorder.

Money as a magnifier

In his book, *Intentional Wealth: How Families Build Legacies of Stewardship and Financial Health,* family wealth consultant Courtney Pullen writes that money tends to reveal the truth of what people are really like. Wealth, he observes, serves 'as an accelerant. No matter what people are like, if you add money, they'll be more that way.'[33] When I work with financial therapy or coaching clients, I frequently see how money reveals what Pullen calls the 'pre-existing fault lines' in both individuals and families. Most of the problems that come to my attention as a wealth psychologist can be viewed as falling under one of four categories:

Overvaluing of money: Manifestations can include over-spending, workaholism, excessive frugality, and high-risk investing. Even though their behaviours may look quite different, people who overvalue money share a belief that *more money = more happiness.* They believe that money promises them a level of security, status and comfort that is to be sought over all else.

Example: Janet and Dave are a very-high-earning couple whose net worth is shrinking alarmingly because of their insatiable desire to always have the best of everything. They see that they are facing an impoverished retirement because of their lifestyle choices. In an effort to make up for the shortfall, they have instructed their advisor to put 100% of their investable assets into high-risk stocks.

Undervaluing of money: Manifestations include chronic under-earning, harmful levels of giving, and lack of savings or investment planning. Clients may believe that they are undeserving of money, or that a desire to have money is somehow sordid, shallow, or selfish.

Example: Viola is a self-employed virtual assistant whose skills are in high demand. She charges a pittance for her work, and is struggling to make ends meet. Her own clients are urging her to raise her rates, but she keeps rejecting their advice. Thinking about or discussing the market value of her work makes her very anxious, so she avoids it, and keeps hoping things will 'just work out'.

Misuse of money in relationships: Manifestations include secret funds, financial exploitation, co-dependency, and use of money to control others. The conflation of money with power, love, or control affects some clients' closest bonds (or even their ability to form them).

Example: Antoine has long been groomed to take over his family's chain of automobile dealerships. He recently disclosed to his parents that he is gay, and that he needs to break off his engagement to a woman they all deeply cherish. His parents are threatening to cut him out of the succession plan if he does not go ahead with the marriage.

Illegal or unethical financial dealings: Manifestations include fraud, tax evasion, theft, and abuse of powers of attorney. The drivers for such behaviours are quite varied, ranging from frank psychopathy to anxious avoidance to a desperate attempt to deal with a shortfall.

Example: *Meghan is the only daughter of a frail, elderly widower. She helps him with all aspects of his life, and has full access to all of his accounts. She recently cashed in $100,000 of her father's investments to pay off her own debts before her husband finds out that she has a gambling problem.*

They're in this thing together – right?

As if it weren't hard enough to deal with one person's money script, along comes another person in the form of a spouse. Couples can have complementary or opposing money scripts. When his belief that 'money will take care of itself' is matched by hers that 'money should not be discussed', a collusion of silence and financial neglect is born. With such a coupling, the consequences may take years to reveal themselves. But when 'I deserve to spend money' marries 'one should never spend frivolously', the fur may begin to fly long before the couple walks down the aisle.

Author and financial therapist Olivia Mellan has observed that 'couples usually polarize around money'.[34] Even if they are quite similar in values and behaviours when they start out together, one partner usually comes to be identified as the 'super' spender/saver/control freak, while the other party ends up trying to create a counterbalance. Conflicts around money, says Mellan, become deeply entrenched over time when couples fail to notice and appreciate the strengths each of them brings to the union.

Financial advice is more apt to be abandoned when it requires cooperation from reluctant or hostile family members. Many an advisor has worked hard to create a sustainable cash flow and expenditure plan with a client, only to have that plan thwarted by the client's free-spending spouse or children.

The things we don't talk about

Children in many Western countries are taught early on not to ask questions about how much people make, or how much things cost. Violating that rule – however innocently – can lead to the kind of emotional reaction that creates an indelible money script within seconds.

These strictures against discussing personal finance make it difficult to open up in circumstances when it would be unwise and unhelpful not to do so – with a prospective marriage partner, for example, or within the family unit. Courtney Pullen writes about the need for families to distinguish between *privacy* and *secrecy* when it comes to household finance. The former, he explains, is simply keeping information within the family that is no one else's business; the latter is too often a conspiracy of silence that prevents healthy financial attitudes and habits from developing.[35]

Given this backdrop of secrecy, it should come as no surprise to learn that clients often do not disclose their financial circumstances fully and frankly with anyone in their life, including the financial professionals they hire. This reticence can show up through delays in signing release forms, in getting paperwork sent over, etc. I have had several advisors tell me of clients who asked them to collude in hiding important aspects of their financial situation from their spouses – secret funds, secret debts, even secret offspring.

The high rates of financial illiteracy

Some years ago, the Canadian government set up a federal task force to look into financial literacy rates, nationwide. It found that 42% of our citizenry did not possess the skills necessary for understanding a basic credit card or phone bill. How, then, do you suppose they would fare in deciphering a typical prospectus or monthly statement from an investment company?

The problem is not that I live in an unusually backward country. The statistics are similarly dismaying in other countries around the world. Since parents often fail to have candid discussions with their children about money matters, and since it is rare for elementary or secondary schools to include lessons on personal finance in their curricula, I am pessimistic that this will change anytime soon.

What this means for the average financial professional is that many clients will be uncomprehending of important aspects of advice they are given. This not only makes it very hard to get truly informed consent, but it also decreases the likelihood that clients will follow through with what they were advised to do.

Painful money legacies

Some clients will arrive at your office with a history of painful dealings with or around money. They may have been the objects of scorn and derision because their families were poor, or they may have been the objects of envy and loathing because their families were rich. They may have been exploited, ripped off, or defrauded by friends, family members, or professionals. They may have been frivolous, imprudent, or neglectful with respect to spending and investing. They may show up with a chip on their shoulder, feeling they have something to prove to you or defend against. Or they may arrive with feelings of profound shame for what they have done or failed to do in their financial lives.

Anna was one such client in my practice. She and her husband came in to try and reverse the escalating debt cycle that was threatening their most cherished life goals. During a homework assignment they had been given to track their expenses, her husband was unintentionally sharp in his criticism of recent expenditures. Usually a bright and ebullient woman, Anna came into our next appointment shut down and spaced out. It took a while for me to recognize that she was not just distracted – she was dissociative. This is a response to extreme stress that is usually rooted in previous trauma. Gentle probing revealed what she had hidden from both me and her husband. We knew that she had grown up in a religious cult that controlled all aspects of its members' lives. What we did not know was the extent to which money had been used as an instrument of control. As a child, she witnessed her parents being publicly shamed for buying her a birthday present without getting permission from the cult leader. The financial and social punishments meted out for this 'sin' lasted weeks, forming the basis for her lifelong financial anxiety and avoidance. Decades later, her husband's criticism of her purchases triggered some very bad memories indeed, and left her temporarily unable to participate meaningfully in the work we had planned to do together.

These kinds of troubled dealings with money often lead people to become financially avoidant and fearful. But at the other end of the spectrum are the clients who have concluded that they are somehow financially invincible, untouchable. They resist buying any kind of insurance because of an inherent belief that bad things simply will not happen to them, or that they will cope with such eventualities as they arise with their usual panache. They are overconfident in their ability to pick winning stocks or turn losing companies around. Attempts to get these 'Invincibles' to engage in a more grounded, considerate approach to their finances is often met with considerable resistance.

Not knowing what to do with clients' anger, tears, or exasperation, advisors often treat client emotions like a nuisance variable or an embarrassment. It feels like nothing more than a hindrance to the real work they're supposed to be doing. This is both naïve and bad form. It increases the odds that the clients will find another advisor. By contrast, a skilled advisor helps to discharge the unhelpful energy that exists around money. This is part of the 'settling' that such clients hope to achieve when they seek advice. Of all the positive benefits of advice outlined in Chapter 3, those pertaining to *encouragement, action,* and a *sense of safety* are most germane to clients with painful money histories.

Some money is different from other money

In the world of arithmetic, one dollar always equals one dollar. But when it comes to the human psyche, it seems that not all dollars are the same. Financial professionals encounter this phenomenon all the time. The 'windfall effect' is perhaps one of the most frequently seen examples. When people receive an infusion of cash that falls outside their regular income stream – a birthday gift, for example, or a tax refund, or a year-end bonus – they tend to treat those dollars as special money. As such, they do different things with that money than they would with a regular pay cheque. Most commonly, they treat themselves and their family members, buying food or gifts or arranging for experiences that are more lavish than usual.

'Mental accounting' is another variant on this phenomenon. For example, many inheritors want inheritance money to be earmarked for special purposes that will somehow memorialize or honour the giver of the gift. My son, for example, wanted to get a special tattoo with his inheritance money from his grandmother. (I'm sure that's just what grandma would have wanted.)

Treating some money as different from other money can be helpful, at times. Earmarking a particular savings account for a home purchase or college fund can be a powerful way to harness the quirk of mental accounting to achieve important personal goals; unfortunately, accountants more often see the downside of this tendency to view some money as special money. 'How many times', they rail, 'do I have to tell clients that their bonus still falls under the heading of 'taxable income' and that they can't spend it all?!!'

Lots of times, apparently.

How scarcity affects the brain

'Poverty makes you stupid' was the headline that came across my computer screen in the fall of 2013. The caption was an unfortunately crass take on the elegant work of behavioural economist Sendhil Mullainathan and cognitive psychologist Eldar Shafir. Their book, *Scarcity: Why Having Too Little Means So Much*, is an intriguing exploration of what happens to people's thinking when they are facing insufficient amounts of any important resource – time, food, and money among them.[36]

Professors Mullainathan and Shafir have amassed strong proof that financial scarcity causes people to hyperfocus on their difficulties in order to find solutions. Such a tunnelling of attention is frequently successful in helping identify solutions for the shortfall, but it comes at a price. The scholars refer to that cost as a 'tax on cognitive bandwidth': that is, a lessening of the mental energy that would otherwise be available for such things as managing mood, resisting distractions, thinking creatively, or fighting off temptations. The hyperfocusing leads to temporary but significant lowering of individuals' IQ test scores (by 13 points, on average). Intriguingly, the scarcity effect can be triggered simply by asking people to *imagine* that they are faced with a situation involving an unexpected bill that is beyond their ability to pay. Whether real or perceived, scarcity takes a bite out of people's neuropsychological resources, not just their financial ones.

How significant is this cognitive tax? Scarcity-induced reductions in IQ are of the same magnitude seen as a result of severe and prolonged sleep deprivation or a moderate brain injury. In real-world situations, such lowered IQ test scores could result in complications ranging from automatic loss of eligibility for elite programming (e.g. consideration for pilot training in the Armed Forces) to inappropriate classification into a mentally handicapped category. Test scores aside, the scarcity effect has been found to render people less able to make prudent spending decisions in its aftermath. When they do get a subsequent infusion of cash after a period of being low on funds, they tend to view the new money as a windfall event, spending excessively on themselves and their family members to make up for the previous period of insufficient resources. In my practice, I've seen such a swing between scarcity and windfall effects across the wealth spectrum – in welfare recipients, in teachers who are paid monthly rather than semi-monthly, and in self-employed people with irregular income streams (farmers and lawyers, for example).

Mullainathan and Shafir found that the loss of bandwidth was a remarkably robust phenomenon. They uncovered it in both imagined and real scenarios of financial privation, in settings as diverse as a New Jersey shopping mall to the farm fields of India. Scarcity, conclude the authors, raises a racket in the brain. Such a racket temporarily diverts other cognitive resources, rendering a person less capable than he or she would otherwise be under conditions of more sustained sufficiency or abundance.

Scarcity in the advisor's office

This scarcity dynamic is often part of the background racket that your clients have been experiencing prior to meeting with you. If you were in the financial planning profession during the last major recession, you would likely have seen demonstrations of the scarcity effect, up close and personal, in many of your clients. The telltale neuropsychological signs would have included greater emotional volatility, short-sightedness, and rigidity, along with a reduced capacity for seeing positive possibilities. Recessions call upon advisors' skills at the personal side of advising in a major way.

But scarcity can be triggered by matters far less obvious and shared than a global recession or widespread financial crisis. It can be sparked by deeply personal events that are the reason the client wants to meet with you: a divorce, a job loss, a cancer diagnosis. It can be set off by hidden factors they do not readily disclose: job insecurity, a midlife crisis, an adult child who is struggling in life. Scarcity has even been found to be triggered by seemingly innocuous experiences in the advisor's own office suite. When waiting room televisions are tuned to financial programmes, for example, clients begin to experience heightened financial anxiety – even on days when the markets are up and the news is good! When emotions about money are running high, your clients may become less cognitively capable than usual.

Is it too late to become a florist?

As the previous pages have demonstrated, the domain of financial advising has particular and peculiar challenges that are simply not present for advice-givers in other fields. That is why, after a day spent dealing with one-too-many financial landmines, many financial professionals start fantasizing about a career change. Admit it, every once in a while you've thought about opening up a surf board concession, a dog-walking business, a knee-capping service. You're in good company.

It is important that you avoid thinking of emotion as an enemy to be kept at bay during the advising process. The goal is not to turn your clients (or yourself) into the actuarial equivalent of the Tin Man from *The Wizard of Oz*. What you want to create is an advising engagement that is generally free from the sway of short-term emotions. In its place is *emotionally intelligent advising*, grounded in a keen appreciation of clients' deeply held values and life aspirations.

Summary

The domain of finance poses special adherence challenges for those who choose to work in the area. Clients arrive at our doors having had a lifetime of being influenced by money in ways both subtle and obvious. There are strong beliefs and values attached to money that are rooted in everything from survival instincts to family legacies to personal triumphs and failures. Some financial circumstances can lead to demonstrable impairment in problem-solving abilities. Advising excellence requires the ability to help clients escape the sway of short-term emotions and tap into deeper levels of motivation and meaning.

Adherence Boosters

1. It is not always easy to avoid the hidden landmines or to uncover the hidden strengths in clients' financial lives. The odds increase significantly, however, if you make attempts

to ask about them! Here are some valuable questions to add to your repertoire. It's important that you listen attentively and explore answers thoughtfully, without any shame or blame or judgment in your responses.

'Have you ever worked with a (*insert your profession here*)? What went well? What didn't go so well?'

'What is happening in your life that led you to contact us now?'

'What aspects of your financial life are you pleased with? What do you do well in terms of earning, saving, investing, and giving? Is there anything you'd like to improve?'

'How would you describe your current relationship with money / your attitude towards money? Has that changed over time? Have you had any bad experiences around money?'

'How comfortable are you talking about money with the people closest to you? How about with me, or with other financial professionals?'

'What do you need to have happen in meetings in order to feel comfortable and productive?'

'What values and beliefs do you have about money that are important for me to understand about you?'

'If you could change one thing about how you deal with money, what would that be? And if you could change anything about your financial circumstances, what would that be?'

'What difference do you suppose these changes would make? Why would they be important to you (your family, your business, etc.)?'

2. Don't just save these questions for your new prospects. Go through the questions above with some of your long-standing clients, too. Whenever I give this assignment to my coaching clients, they always uncover new and valuable things about clients they've known for many years.

3. Alternatively, whenever you bring a new team member on board, have them ask such questions of your existing clients prior to meeting with you. By virtue of their status as newbies, a new team member can ask questions that might seem naïve or odd coming from longstanding team members; in return, the new team member is apt to receive answers that are correspondingly more candid or fresh or updated. New team members can help to counteract the familiarity bias that can creep in over time, a bias that can lead to dangerously unchecked assumptions.

4. Some clients need more support around overcoming painful money histories than you can offer them. Be sure you have the name of some individual and family therapists in your area for clients who want help in creating healthier relationships to and around money. There are also many

good money coaches available. They often use video or teleconference technologies to connect with clients, and are thus able to work with people around the globe.

No matter the territory involved, there are some kinds of advice that are much easier to follow than others. Within your own practice, you will likely have encountered the fact that some tasks are more routinely neglected or rejected by clients than others. In the next chapter, as we turn to the 'A' (which stands for 'Advice Characteristics') in the FACTS model, we'll explore why that is.

Chapter 5

What Makes Some Advice Harder to Take Than Others

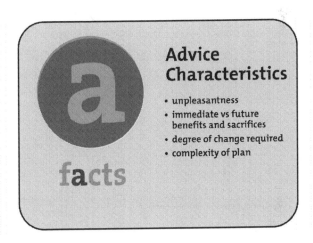

a

facts

Advice Characteristics

- unpleasantness
- immediate vs future benefits and sacrifices
- degree of change required
- complexity of plan

The scene in the lecture hall was one of happy chaos. My colleague, Dr. Jason Ediger, had been tasked with helping a class of medical students understand why patients so often fail to comply with their doctor's advice. And he knew that he would be faced with students' lack of life experience and general information overload. So he did what every good teacher does: He armed himself with candy and a healthy dose of mischief, and he went to work ...

...which explains some of the bizarre things I observed when I arrived at the class. There were students popping up at random intervals performing the chicken dance. There were students using teeth and nails to get layers of packing tape off packages of candy. There were students with looks of utter revulsion on their faces, trying to make themselves swallow black jellybeans and wasabi peas. All of this, while Professor Ediger lectured on, heedless of the chaos.

What I soon learned was that all of the students had been given individualized assignments at the outset of the class. In addition to being responsible for learning the lecture material, the students were tasked with doing certain things at designated times and in specific ways. Unbeknownst to them, the tasks they were assigned were all designed to simulate some aspect of medical advice that is frequently hard to implement. For example:

> The tightly wrapped candy packages were meant to simulate how hard it is for many elderly patients to deal with child-proof packaging.

> The wasabi peas and black jellybeans were meant to demonstrate how much willpower is required for chronically ill patients to take unpleasant medications.

> The chicken dance was meant to alert them to the social discomfort experienced by many teenage diabetics who have to test their blood sugars at school or eat differently from their peers.

And on it went. When surveyed afterwards, only a small percentage of the students had been able or willing to fully comply with the complex set of instructions they'd been given. As for their mastery of the content of Professor Ediger's lecture, given while all the shenanigans were going on? Well, let's just say their grades on the ensuing surprise quiz weren't up to their usual standards of excellence. They were all relieved to learn that the marks wouldn't be counted.

Those soon-to-be physicians learned some lessons that day they'll not soon forget. Among them:

1. No matter how motivated or smart the advice-seeker may be, there's a lot that can get in the way of follow-through.
2. Trying to comply with a complex set of instructions places a tax on intellectual and attentional resources, getting in the way of other important things (such as ongoing learning).
3. The chicken dance is remarkably undignified.

In the previous chapter, we reviewed some of the reasons why financial advice is particularly hard to take. We considered the unconscious money scripts that can be at work in our clients, and the disordered behaviours and troubled relationships that they can help to create. We reviewed how low levels of financial literacy, lack of experience in talking about money, and financial scarcity can all pose additional complications.

But even when recommendations have nothing to do with money, they can still be hard for people to implement. Whether we're talking about money or medicine, fitness or food, there is some advice that's simply harder to take than others. The chart below shows what differentiates the two:

Easy-to-follow advice	Hard-to-follow advice
Single behaviour	Broader lifestyle change
Short-term	Long-term
Provides relief of current problem	Preventative in nature
Easy to implement	Complex or painful
Highly supported or supervised	High degree of self-reliance
Culturally common / discreet	Visibly different

Let's 'warm up' by examining a few adherence situations from outside the domain of finance. Read the case studies in this chapter in light of the above chart, and consider whether the directives given to the individuals fall under the Easy or Hard columns.

Scenario 1: The executive physical

As a condition of their continued employment, executives of large companies are often required to undergo comprehensive annual health examinations. A private health care facility has been contracted to provide these physicals. Every year, a case manager calls the executives, reminds them of their contractual requirement, and books the appointment. An e-mail reminder is sent out two days before the appointment, requiring confirmation of their intention to attend. A car and driver are dispatched to the company to pick up the executives and return them to work. Afterward, the case manager forwards a confidential report to the personnel committee of the company's board.

Is complying with this requirement an Easy or Hard task for the executives?

This scenario meets most of the Easy criteria outlined above. The executives need only submit to the physical. It's a brief involvement, relatively painless, carried out in private, with multiple layers of support and accountability mechanisms. The only one of the Easy criteria that it fails to meet is that it does not necessarily provide relief from any discomfort. It does, however, provide an opportunity for the executive to discuss any health concerns they might have. Under such conditions, the compliance rates approach 100%.

Scenario 2: The 'You have diabetes!' wake-up call

Next, consider the challenges in dealing with a health problem that is reaching alarming proportions in North America.

A man has just been diagnosed with advanced Type II diabetes. He is already showing signs of serious complications of the disease, including reduced circulation to his feet and changes to his vision. He is given a new daily routine that involves taking four types of medication, checking blood sugar levels morning and night, losing 80 pounds, and getting his blood pressure under control. He is instructed in foot care and advised to have vision checks done twice a year. He is given multiple brochures to explain the disease. One of the pamphlets includes the phone number for the clinic's dietitian, whom he is advised to call for help with dietary changes.

You can confidently assume that such a barrage of directives falls under the Hard-to-follow category. The advice requires widespread lifestyle changes that must be enacted from Now until Kingdom Come. Those changes are complex and unpleasant to implement, and will require him to alter his intake and lifestyle in ways that will be apparent to those around him. If he is lucky, he will receive some support from his family in making the necessary lifestyle changes – perhaps they will offer to go to the gym with him, or resolve to improve their eating habits, too; nevertheless, the required changes will require a considerable degree of self-reliance and willpower for this man. The compliance rates in such conditions plummet to between 7% and 30%, with the higher percentages associated exclusively with clinics that provide more frequent supervision and check-ins.

HEADS UP!

In my consultation and coaching practice, I am frequently called upon to help financial professionals deal with vexing client situations. The greatest frustration seems to be elicited by clients who are not adhering to agreed-upon action plans. Insurance specialists can't get back the paperwork needed to buy a policy demanded by a client's business partner. Credit counsellors have clients who are three months in arrears on their repayments, and nowhere to be found. Financial planners bear witness to trust fund recipients who won't rein in their prolific overspending, despite their express avowals to do so.

Consider again the chart that outlines the characteristics of advice that is easy versus challenging:

Easy-to-follow advice	Hard-to-follow advice
Single behaviour	Broader lifestyle change
Short-term	Long-term
Provides relief of current problem	Preventative in nature
Easy to implement	Complex or painful
Highly supported or supervised	High degree of self-reliance
Culturally common / discreet	Visibly different

Typical financial counsel tends to have more in common with the right-hand column than the left. Much of what we educate our clients to do is profoundly countercultural. We ask them to resist the pervasive messages of advertisers to spend freely, and instead tell them to invest disposable income now so that they can reap benefits that may be decades in coming. Rather than providing relief of a current pain point, our best counsel is often aimed at preventing future problems. Our meetings may obligate them to contemplate unpleasant outcomes like death and disability, or to have difficult conversations with family members and business partners. They may find themselves having to persist through feeling 'stupid' or 'out of their league' as they make decisions about insurance, investments, and estate decisions.

Heads up, advisors! Know from the outset that you've got a significant adherence challenge on your hands *because of the nature of the advice you have to give.* Regardless of the skill or sensitivity with which you make recommendations, some of your advice is a lot harder to swallow than a pill.

Let's examine of couple of the common scenarios that cause difficulty for financial professionals.

Scenario 3: Keeping track

A heavily indebted client has reached out to her credit union for help in addressing her debt load. She indicates she has no idea how much the non-discretionary costs of her life are. After confirming she has a basic knowledge of how to use Excel spreadsheets, the credit union employee gives her a template and requests that she track her expenses for the next month. Before she leaves, they set up the next appointment.

Is this advice generally of the 'Easy' or the 'Hard' variety?

If you are in the habit of giving this assignment, you will know that the adherence rates are middling, at best. Tracking does not provide a quick fix for the problem of indebtedness, nor for the accompanying financial stress and scarcity involved. Although 'tracking expenses' might seem like a single behaviour, in truth it involves multiple steps for the client: being conscious of the fact that she's spending money; asking for a receipt; storing and later retrieving that receipt; signing up for online banking; setting aside the time to make entries; and doing the entries frequently enough so that the process is not excessively daunting. If the client has been actively avoiding an examination of her finances (for example, because she is anxious or ashamed), this exercise can be quite distressing. Finally, in the month that she is left on her own to track her expenses, the client may forget important aspects of the assignment or become utterly discouraged. Wealth advisors, bank officers, and credit counselling agencies alike report to me that they experience a lot of 'no shows' for that next appointment.

Scenario 4: Oh boy! Let's talk about death!

As part of doing comprehensive financial plans with her clients, a planner requires that clients get a will, power of attorney, and health care directive in place. Her clientele are primarily young professionals who have not yet taken care of these matters. She provides them with simple reading materials that explain the need for each of these documents. She gives them the names of three estate attorneys she knows to be personable, proficient, and ethical. She requests that they get these documents done within the next three months.

The preventative nature of this advice, combined with the unpleasant emotions it evokes and the extra expenses involved, frequently results in people procrastinating on such matters – sometimes for years. The planner in the current scenario has done some good things by providing reading materials and the names of competent attorneys in her community. Without more direct involvement, however, she is fighting an uphill battle. The percentage of North Americans without a will has hovered around the 60% mark for decades. The statistics for health care directives are harder to uncover (largely because of varying standards as to what they must include), but it seems that 70%

to 80% of the general population is without one. Young, healthy individuals are especially loath to embrace these tasks.

It will be important to ascertain what the client *is* prepared to act on with respect to these recommendations. Depending on what she learns in response to taking her client through the Readiness Questions outlined in the next chapter, the planner might be well advised to back off on the rather daunting demand for all three documents to be produced in the next three months. She might find she gets more traction by mitigating the statistically greatest risks faced by younger clients – for example, ensuring that disability insurance is in place, and that beneficiaries have been designated on all appropriate documents in their workplaces. Success in these easier tasks often boosts adherence with harder ones, later on.*

Summary

No matter the domain involved, it is evident that some directives are more readily agreed to than others. Under the 'Hard-to-follow' category are recommendations requiring widespread, long-term behaviour changes that must be enacted without direct supervision or support. Adherence is further complicated when advice is preventative in nature, when it

---

* This approach benefits from something called 'Commitment and Consistency' principles. When people first commit to one small step, and then are given opportunities to engage in similar, related actions, the uptake is usually greater than if they were presented with the entire array of opportunities at once.

requires painful or unpleasant tasks, and when it is out of step with what is normative for the client's social circle or culture.

Adherence Boosters

1. **Switch columns:** Whenever possible, alter the 'Hard-to-follow' elements of the advice you have to give so that it falls more readily under the 'Easy-to-follow' column. Take each row of the chart above and consider how you might change your advice delivery with clients who are obviously bogged down or stuck in carrying out tasks assigned to them. The remaining Adherence Boosters are all examples of how you might do this.

2. **Turn multi-step advice into a series of single behaviours**: With my own overspending clients, for example, I frequently roll out my interventions as though I were doing the Dance of the Seven Veils. I first check whether they are in agreement with doing (a fairly easy) first step:

   Success Step 1: Turn off 1-click ordering on all devices.

   When they confirm that they have taken that step, I e-mail them the next step:

   Success Step 2: Get all your bank accounts online.

   When that is done, I move them on to the third step:

   Success Step 3: Look at account transactions every day.

Even though such steps are unnecessarily small for some clients (who would therefore be given more to do at a time), they work magic for people who have been financially avoidant. They result in a series of rapid successes for people more accustomed to being criticized than encouraged. When we get to the end of the sequence of small steps, such clients are confidently and competently tracking their finances.

3. **Use short-term current commitments to eliminate the need for ongoing steps in the future:** Many advisors assist their clients to set up pre-authorized monthly deposits into their investment accounts. A one-time minor task (filling out paperwork) removes the need for them to summon up the energy and willpower to repeatedly send the monies, month after month. This is a great model to try and implement in other areas – for example, fixing a price point at which stocks will be sold in the future, or pre-committing to having a certain percentage of future wage increases go into retirement savings.*

4. **Each time you meet, ask the client what the desired outcome of the meeting is:** The content of your

---

* People will often pre-commit to future savings rates that are considerably more generous than what they are currently prepared to set aside. If you encounter resistance to your calculations regarding the amount of money clients need to be saving in order to reach their goals, try moving the start date out six months in the future and getting the paperwork set up in advance. That figure becomes the new default option, and is much more likely to be adhered to.

recommendations may still need to be largely preventative in nature, but asking this question alerts both of you to the *current* issue that he or she wants to address. This turns even the most prevention-oriented session (e.g. setting up a retirement strategy for 30 years down the road) into something that solves a current concern or pain point (i.e. their need to feel confident that they have taken appropriate action and are in expert hands).

5. **Ask the client to predict what aspects of things they are most likely to struggle with:** Their self-knowledge is apt to be better than your good guesses. The things that a professional engineer might find complex and painful may well be different from the things that a professional dancer might find complex and painful – and both may be very different from what you would have predicted.

6. **Brainstorm with them regarding how the assigned task could be made easier or more palatable:** Do they want to get the hardest task over with first, or work up to it? Is there anything that you and your team could take over for them? Is there someone who might be willing to pitch in to make the task less onerous? Could they get someone else to take over their other chores or obligations while they work on this particular task? Do not let them leave the meeting without having a plan in place to get through the hard tasks.

7. **Offer more tactical support and encouragement than you think is necessary:** There will always be competing demands on your clients' time and energy. Many of them

are going through major life transitions that render them fatigued, grieving, stressed, and depleted. Support from you and your team in the form of frequent scheduled check-ins helps clients to remember their commitments and to persist with goal attainment. Be sure to communicate small wins and successes along the way, e.g. 'You're more than halfway to your retirement goal!' or 'You have enough money in the business to hire an additional employee.'

8. **Have a healthy respect for the limits of memory:** One of the leading causes of unintentional non-adherence is garden-variety forgetting. You can boost the likelihood of follow-through just by applying a few commitment strategies and memory prompts. For example, having people write down their own next appointment date (versus simply accepting an appointment card from you) decreases the rate of no-shows by 18%.[37] Since a combination of written and spoken information is more memorable than either method alone, make a point of using both.

9. **Ask people to commit, out loud, to the next action steps:** Securing a verbal commitment is a more successful strategy than simply handing them your handwritten note of what to do next. I routinely ask my clients, 'Tell me what we agreed would be the next step, and why. What is the date by which you are committing to getting this done?'

10. **Whenever possible, send a quick e-mail that outlines what each of you has committed to do after the meeting, and**

by when: This provides a further memory prompt and an additional source of encouragement to get into action.

11. **Let people know that you will report back to them regarding your commitments:** When you call or message them regarding what you have done, you can quickly check in with how they're doing. This gives you a chance to remind, encourage, or problem-solve, as required.

In the next two chapters, we turn our attention to the 'C' in the FACTS model: that is, to matters that are more directly related to the clients themselves – for example, their understanding, motivation, confidence, and energy. I'll present strategies for improving their ability to implement your recommendations.

Client Characteristics (Part 1): Working with the Horse You've Got

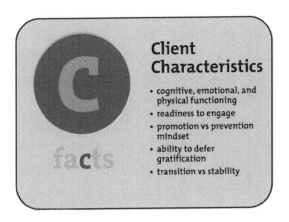

Client Characteristics

- cognitive, emotional, and physical functioning
- readiness to engage
- promotion vs prevention mindset
- ability to defer gratification
- transition vs stability

O n a recent plane trip, I sat next to a man who owned a number of racehorses. I learned from him that the decision to purchase a racehorse is a big one, with considerations of lineage, conformation, and past race performance looming large during the selection process. Having made a purchase, however, the owner does not simply stick the prize thoroughbred in the stall and wait until race day to bring it out. Instead, he starts to train the horse shortly after it settles in. Observations are made about what calms or stresses the animal; an exercise regimen is instituted; dietary issues are monitored and adjusted. Winning horses, I learned, are both born *and* created.

All of us are welcome to try and pre-select the 'winning horse' when we interview prospective clients. But once they become our clients, we need to redefine our objectives, thinking less like a gambler and more like a trainer. We need to figure out how to work with the horse we've got.

The holy grail of adherence research

Decades of research have gone into trying to identify the traits of people who are most likely to be 'bad' patients or clients – that is, the people who can be counted on to *not* comply with the directives they are given. The driving notion has been that, if we could identify and avoid such people, we would have a much more productive and satisfying work life! It's a compelling idea that becomes even more attractive when we are in the midst of working with someone whose non-adherence is putting everything (including our own composure) at risk.

But the quest to identify non-adherent personality types has not been a great success. That's because the likelihood of adherence tends to be:

> *Fluctuating* – changeable over time, depending on such things as conviction, memory, energy levels, etc.

> *Environmentally influenced* – changeable across different situations, depending on such things as social support, peer pressure, and external demands.

Domain-specific – changeable from one area of life to another (e.g. one can have a firm commitment to not talking on the cell phone while driving, while simultaneously being grievously negligent about cleaning the furnace filters).

That makes sense, no? Can you think of anyone who is globally non-adherent – that is, who fails to comply with any directives, ever? Even the most oppositional or disagreeable person you can call to mind is still apt to fall in line with many basic rules or guidelines, e.g. stopping at red lights, arriving at work on time, etc. The research shows clearly that all people 'cherry pick' which directives they will comply with or try out, based on considerations that extend well beyond personality styles.

You know it's going to be challenging when ...

It turns out that there are, indeed, some good predictors of non-adherence that have to do directly with the client – it's just that they aren't usually rooted in fixed, unyielding personality characteristics. The most reliable client-centric predictors of non-adherence tend to be behavioural and attitudinal, not characterological. If you want to get better at predicting non-adherence, look for the following indicators:

A history of rejecting similar advice: It is a truism in psychology that *the best predictor of future behaviour is past behaviour.* This is why it is so important that you ask clients about their previous successes and challenges within the specific domain of money management. You should also ask them about their past experiences of investing and working with financial advisors (suggested questions in this regard are found in Chapter 5). To my mind, this real-life experience is much more important to truly knowing your client than much of what is contained in standard 'Know Your Client' regulatory forms (e.g. risk tolerance estimates that often are pure conjecture). Just remember that a history of non-adherence in one aspect of their financial lives is not an automatic indicator that they will be a 'problem client'. (That new 60-year-old client who has repeatedly put off getting a will in place may nevertheless be a disciplined saver and a thoughtful investor.) But a history of non-adherence does give you a 'heads up' that additional support and planning may be required in domain-specific areas.

A large discrepancy in opinion between you and them: Remember the list of reasons that people seek advice in the first place? It all boils down to wanting to feel more *settled* as a result of having sought expert opinion. When the advisor and the advisee are worlds apart in their view of the problem and/or solution, that is profoundly *unsettling*. Little surprise, then, that people are more than twice as likely to follow through with professional advice that confirms their pre-existing opinions. This effect (which, as we have already noted, is known as the confirmation bias) has been found to be strongest in emotion-laden domains such as religion or politics, or when people have a strong underlying motive to believe one way versus the other.[38] I think we can agree that the domain of money might just rival religion and politics in terms of emotion and motive-generating potential.

The presence of limiting beliefs: It is not unusual for a client to tell me things such as, 'I'm no good with money' or 'I'm a financial idiot'. Such deeply entrenched aspects of self-identity are a sure tip-off that there is an underlying money script at work (see Chapter 4 if you need a refresher on money scripts). Among the most limiting of beliefs is a person's conviction that he or she can do nothing to create a different outcome: 'That's just the way it is for me.' Treat all such disclosures with respect, and make note of them in the client's files. As much as it may pain you, *do not argue* with their defeatist self-appraisals, or attempt to provide them with evidence to the contrary. Instead, simply voice your commitment to providing them with better experiences of dealing with money. Review and implement the strategies on dealing with ambivalence that are presented later in this chapter.

Low ability to delay gratification: This is probably as close to a personality trait as you will find with respect to adherence – it is more deeply entrenched than most of the other predictors, and can be particularly challenging to overcome. Human beings are hard-wired to repeat actions that make them feel good. This makes us all suckers for here-and-now rewards. Over time, most people learn strategies for eschewing immediate gratification for the sake of achieving greater long-term rewards. Many of our most frustrating, stress-inducing clients have not developed those strategies. The 'tells' for such a problem include not only such obvious indicators as high levels of consumer debt and low savings rates, but also subtler signs such as excessive giving (often to offspring) or constant postponement of important meetings.

Not believing there is a problem: On occasion, you will find yourself in the presence of clients who seem intent on fiddling while Rome is burning: that is, they seem completely unconcerned about key aspects of their financial situation that desperately need to be addressed. These clients usually come in at the behest of a *concerned someone else* –perhaps a bank officer, a family member, or a Human Resources manager. The challenge for the advisor, once again, is to keep from arguing with them in order to convince them that there *is* a problem. You need to determine why they agreed to visit you in the first place. Although they may have come in simply to get someone off their back, you may be able to leverage that desire and nudge them towards taking a few steps in the right direction. Over the course of their meeting with you, they may encounter revelatory new information, or experience a sense of support and connection that leaves them hopeful about different possibilities for their lives. They may have come in believing *there is no problem*, but you need not conclude *there is no point*. You can be a catalyst for change.

Lacklustre motivation: Research from the field of positive psychology makes it clear that high levels of motivation are important in goal achievement. Especially if the goal is a daunting one, folks need to get in touch with why they want to experience or create something different in their financial life; without such motivation, they will fail to launch, or fizzle out shortly after starting. That motivation needs to be deeply personal if it is to propel behaviour change. Highly enthusiastic advisors can inadvertently cause problems in this regard, as they are able to create a superficial 'Yes Set' in clients using persuasive arguments and lots of encouragement. But acquiescence or intellectual assent is no substitute for heartfelt, personal reasons for change.

Insufficient preparedness: I am an avid armchair adventurer. I love to read stories of ultra-marathoners, or assaults on Everest (and my physique is proof positive that I am happier to read about them than I am to emulate them!). What I have learned from the travails of others boils down to this: All the motivation in the world will not make up for a lack of preparedness. Highly motivated clients with the best intentions can fail simply because they do not have the right supports in place. They often go off, half-cocked, without contemplating what they will need to reach their goals. One of the jobs of a financial advice-giver is to help clients identify, ahead of time, what is likely to trip them up and what is needed to buoy them up.

What I learned from a knock on the noggin

I heard the cries before I saw the problem. My five-year-old niece lay crying on the pavement, her legs pinned underneath her bicycle and her hand pressed to a nasty gash on the back of her head. It took some time to extricate her and get her cleaned up and settled down, but eventually I got around to an important question:

> 'Honey, I reminded you this morning to wear your helmet. I even put it on your bike seat for you! So why weren't you wearing it?'

And the answer came with all of the honesty I'd come to expect from her:

'I know you told me to wear my helmet, Auntie Moira.
But I never said I would.'

Hmm – she had me there, alright. I had blithely assumed that the compelling and authoritative nature of my advice, combined with how easy I'd made it for her to follow, would be all that was necessary to create an afternoon free of neurological incidents. But I had neglected a few key ingredients in that recipe. Chief among them? Her buy-in.

Even though the blood stains eventually wore off the sidewalk, the lesson I learned that day proved to be indelible. *There can be no good advice without agreement from the advisee.*

In medical circles, this lesson is known as the 'Principle of Readiness'. Teachings on how to assess and increase readiness now feature prominently in most health care training programmes. It's time that those teachings made their way to the financial domain. I believe that the failure to ensure client readiness is the single biggest preventable contributor to the problem of financial non-adherence.

In this chapter, I will share with you a highly effective process for ensuring client readiness.[39] It involves asking a few simple questions of your client. But first, let's begin with *why* you should do this. What difference does it make? Assessing readiness brings many advantages to you. Among them:

- It prevents wasted efforts, and associated wastes of time, energy and money.

- It preserves positive relationships.
- It avoids client discouragement.
- It facilitates the emergence of better solutions than either one of you could come up with on your own.
- It conveys the message that clients can disagree with you without being labelled as 'disagreeable'.
- It reduces the number of evil thoughts about non-adherent clients that you'll later have to atone for.

Assessing readiness is a three-step process. It involves determining that the clients are in agreement with a proposed course of action, harnessing their motivation to act on it, and ensuring that they have a high degree of confidence in a good outcome. Accordingly, there are three main questions that you should be asking anytime you expect a client to do anything of substance in follow-up to a meeting with you. As you will see, the questions not only help you determine the client's readiness for change – they can also increase it.

Step 1: Ensure that you have mutual agreement on what to do next

You may possess superior technical knowledge, but clients have superior knowledge of their own circumstances, desires, and level of energy. In terms of implementation, their knowledge trumps yours every time. This was the critical step that I skipped with my niece on that fateful day. If I'd taken the time to ask, I would have found out that she had absolutely no intention of complying with the directive I'd given her to wear her helmet. (Her princess hair barrettes, it turns out, would have been obscured by the helmet, and she was having none of that.)

To find out whether your advice is landing on receptive ears, start with this first query:

Readiness Question 1: How would you feel about (insert recommended action here)?
e.g. How would you feel about setting up that family trust as we discussed? Working out a tax repayment schedule? Getting your wills and estate plan in place?

Variations on this question include:

What do you think should happen as a result of our discussion today?

Does this seem like the best next step, or is there something more important you'd like to do instead?

Given what you said you wanted to have come out of this meeting, does it make sense to be taking this step?

Notice that these questions do not assume that you know best. They invite the client to bring forth ideas of their own. They reflect the very real possibility that the client might have different opinions about what the next steps should be, and that those opinions have merit.

If you do not have agreement that this would be a good course of action to pursue, do not press on with the next steps. Instead, find out if there is something definite the client would prefer to do instead. See whether you can come up with an agreed-upon next step. Then repeat Question 1 to clarify you're on the same page.

AMBIVALENCE ALERT: If you are being met with a high degree of equivocation about your proposed plan of action, you will be sorely tempted to keep adding more information or to increase the persuasiveness of your reasoning. This runs a high risk of two undesirable scenarios: forcing the clients' objections underground; or having them repeatedly remind themselves of their reasons for not moving ahead. Both scenarios decrease the likelihood of subsequent engagement and adherence. The best choice at this point is to welcome the ambivalence into the room. Emphasize that it is their right to not follow your advice.

'You're not quite sure a family trust is right for your situation. Tell me about that. It is your right to decide what to do, regardless.'

'It seems that part of you wants to move ahead with a plan for tax repayment, but part of you would prefer not to. I'd really like to understand both parts. It'll be up to you to decide.'

'I can see that you're trying to figure out the best thing to do. It seems it's really important to you that you finish up your estate planning, but in the past you've always stopped midway through. Am I understanding this correctly?'

All behaviour has advantages, even if they're not apparent or important to an outside observer. People who are being presented with an option to do things differently need time to sift through the pros and cons of changing, and to get to a point where they can shift their decisional balance by tapping into their own deeply felt motivation. An overzealous advisor can tip the balance in the wrong direction by threatening their autonomy, ridiculing their opinions, or making dire predictions about the negative consequences that will befall them. Resist the urge; instead, roll with the ambivalence. The ensuing discussion will pay dividends.

Step 2: Harness motivation by tapping into purpose

Author and TED Talk favourite Simon Sinek emphasizes the advantages of getting people in touch with their deepest reasons for doing things. In his book, *Start with Why,* Sinek discredits the notion that people can be motivated from the outside in. Rather, he contends, 'People are either motivated or they are not.' The real task, he argues, is to help them figure out the *why* that generates such motivation. Get them in touch with a vision they can believe in, Sinek promises, and they'll have all the motivation they need.[40] (For example, had I tapped into my niece's desire to keep her princess hair barrettes free of blood, she likely would have worn the helmet.)

Asking people about their deepest motivation to engage in a task helps both them and you. They develop a strong attachment to the plan, and you get the opportunity to understand what makes them tick. As a result, the bond between you is strengthened, and becomes a further source of encouragement in and of itself. Strongly motivated clients are more likely to initiate action and persist with it; those with lacklustre motivation are frequently unable to get much past the starting gate.

You can help clients harness their motivation by making the following inquiry:

Readiness Question 2: If you decided to carry out this step, how would it benefit you?

Related questions include:

What difference would it make if you succeeded in this?

Why would that be important to you?

What would life be like if you didn't do this?

What good things could this help bring to pass?

What bad outcomes would this help avoid?

What you want to have emerge in this step is a number of emotionally satisfying benefits that are highly personalized, not abstract or general in nature. Answers such as, 'It's the right thing to do' or 'It would improve my life' are only surface-level responses. They do not typically lead to the benefits outlined above. You need to help them get in touch with the deeper levels of meaning that will help them to persist even when the task is unpleasant.

Marshall Goldsmith has been hailed as one of the most influential business thinkers and coaches on the planet. Goldsmith is in such demand now that he only coaches people in the upper echelons of business, government, and NGOs, people whose expertise is already extraordinarily well-developed and highly recognized. Notwithstanding their demonstrated track record of success, these Fortune 500 CEOs and 5-Star Generals are constantly being called upon to dig deeper and do better. In order to help them get there, Goldsmith often takes them through five or six iterations of the questions listed above. He knows when they have tapped into the right kind of motivation when there are tears in their eyes, or when a profound stillness settles over them.

Not all advice-giving situations warrant this kind of deep inquiry. It would be patently absurd to take clients through such a process when they are clearly already engaged and convinced of the benefits of the advice. For those who are daunted or dubious, however, such inquiry can move them along the spectrum from 'Uncommitted' to 'Deeply Committed'.

Some clients will express their motivation in positive terms, citing things they'd like to create or bring about or experience ('I want to create an ease around money that will make our home life peaceful'). Other clients will express their vision in terms of negative outcomes that they'd like to prevent from happening, citing things that they want to avoid or steer away from ('I want to make sure that my wife never has to struggle when I'm gone'). The first approach has been dubbed *promotion focus*; the second, *prevention focus*. Neither one is superior to the other when it emerges directly from the client.* Allow your client's focus, not yours, to be the predominant one. Use their language, not your own, when reminding them on future occasions of why they are doing what they are doing.

AMBIVALENCE ALERT: People may have trouble envisioning the direct benefits of the advice. This is often true of ambivalent clients. You can help to shift the decisional balance by helping them to consider even the *possibility* of good things happening as a result of making some changes.

'You've helped me to understand why it's hard for you to start that tax repayment process. If something were to change, and you did feel ready to get started, what do you think you might get out of taking this step?'

'If you did decide to get that estate plan in place (and I'm not saying you will), how might that work to your advantage?'

Note once again that you are constantly reinforcing their right to make a different decision than the one you're recommending. Rather than trying to convince them of the benefits of changing, you are helping them to try on a

---

* When it comes to being influenced by outside sources, however, people tend to pay more attention to negative information than to positive, and to act on it more readily. Accordingly, when people ask you directly for *your* take on things, and when you wish to influence them in a certain direction, you may want to give more weight in your responses to the downside information than to the upside.

new possibility, and then to discern whether this is the right decision at the right time. This shifts the dynamic considerably. Instead of seeing you as a debating partner or a judge whom they must convince of the validity of their arguments *against* changing, they begin to get in touch with their own valid arguments *for* changing.

Step 3: Boost self-efficacy

People with low motivation often fail to launch – that is why Step 2 is important.

People with low self-efficacy fail to stay in orbit – that is why Step 3 is recommended.

A few pages back, I wrote that the best predictor of *future behaviour* is often *past behaviour*. That holds true for many situations, much of the time. Taken too far, however, that fact can lead to a kind of pessimism or cynicism about the likelihood of people ever changing. The wonderful thing about our work is that we get to see change happening all the time! On a regular basis, people *can* and *do* break harmful habits, improve unsatisfying relationships, and turn around underperforming track records.

Let's take a different approach to predicting the future by changing the question slightly:

What is the best predictor of *changed* behaviour?

The answer to that question is *self-efficacy,* or confidence in one's ability to achieve important outcomes. If people don't believe that they can do what it takes to reach their goals, they are not likely to engage in the series of steps needed to prepare for, initiate, and sustain the changes they need to make. They'll over-react to foreseeable setbacks, and deflate like a pricked balloon. This holds true as much in the domain of finance as in other domains of life.[41]

As helping professionals who know that we share responsibility for adherence, it is our job to help boost our clients' self-efficacy. The final Readiness Question is a great step in that direction:

Readiness Question 3: If you decided to go ahead with this step, how confident are you that you could do it?

You can explore their confidence (or lack thereof) with further probing:

What contributes to your level of confidence?

Have you ever done anything like this before? How did that go?

What do you think could make it easier to succeed at this task?

What is likely to get in the way? How do you see yourself getting past that?

What kinds of support would help you to keep going when the going gets tough?

These explorations help to create a sense of confidence that is grounded and reality-based.

I frequently come across life coaches and business leaders who insist that asking people to forecast obstacles only serves to increase their likelihood of encountering them. This is a misinterpretation of the scientific findings that have emerged from such fields as motivational interviewing and positive psychology. High performance is not enhanced by rosy techniques such as visualizing oneself executing a flawless performance and standing on the gold medal podium; rather, high performance is maximized by mental rehearsing of rapid recovery from stumbles or falls.

Similarly, strong self-efficacy is not about superficial positive thinking, or a refusal to consider the obstacles ahead. Instead, it's about knowing that one is equipped to meet the challenges that arise. Think of it this way: If you had to choose, would you rather set out to climb Mount Everest alongside a Sherpa who is really positive, or alongside a Sherpa who is really prepared? I suspect you would join me in choosing the latter.

Some days, being a financial professional is a lot like being a Sherpa. Fortunately, you don't have to choose between being positive or prepared. You can show up as both, modelling and teaching the habits that allow your clients to be likewise. If you know of important challenges that they haven't thought of (e.g. legal requirements, cash flow issues, etc.), you will need to bring them to their attention … and then you will need to help identify solutions sufficient to address the problem. This is what helps create the settled state that is the ultimate goal of all advice-seekers.

AMBIVALENCE ALERT: Low confidence is one of the chief reasons that people stay stuck with the status quo. You can enhance self-efficacy by getting people to pay attention to those areas where they do have confidence, or where they have watched someone else succeed. You can also provide a nudge in the direction of change by highlighting the temporary nature of the problems they are anticipating.

Why haven't you completely given up on the possibility that you could experience something better?

What would be a step you could take that you DO feel ready for?

Is there anybody you know of who has been able to do the things you'd like to do? What do you suppose allowed them to do that? Is that something you could try to do, too?

What would be the first small indicator that you were on the way to succeeding?

How willing are you to increase your burden temporarily in order to improve your life in the long run?

Summary

Clients vary in terms of their willingness and ability to implement the advice they have sought from you. Negative prognostic indicators include a history of rejecting or abandoning similar advice, ho-hum feelings towards the plan, and inadequate preparedness.

There are three questions that allow you to quickly assess and increase a client's readiness to carry out a recommended plan of action. They are:

- How would you feel about (insert recommended action here)?
- If you decided to carry out this step, how would it benefit you?
- If you decided to go ahead with this step, how confident are you that you could do it?

Adherence Boosters

1. It is important to go through the Readiness Questions before you conclude that your advice is timely, desirable, and implementable. Failure to ensure readiness is a major contributor to non-adherence. Unless you receive an unambiguous green light on each of these three questions, you do not have a truly 'ready' client. It's better to go with an imperfect Plan B that the client is excited and confident about than to insist on a perfect Plan A that will lie unimplemented.

2. All advice-givers need to be wary about engaging in debate with ambivalent clients. It runs the joint risks of entrenching their commitment to *not* changing and of turning you into the opposition. Work on increasing your comfort and willingness to accept the ambivalence. Help such clients come up with their own reasons for changing rather than convincing them of the validity of yours.

3. When identifying likely barriers to success, be aware that many a plan is ruined when clients rely too heavily on their own willpower. Do not underestimate the environmental and social influences on a client's behaviour. Whenever possible, harness them to boost the likelihood of success (more on this in Chapter 8).

Among the chief benefits of professional advice outlined in Chapter 2 were increases in confidence, the provision of encouragement, and a swifter path to action. The disciplined application of the Readiness Questions process helps you to provide all three benefits while also boosting the likelihood of follow-through. It pays extra dividends when you encounter the common problem of mental depletion, seen most reliably in people going through prolonged life transitions. This is explored in the next chapter.

Chapter 7

Client Characteristics (Part 2): How to Help When Life Packs a Wallop

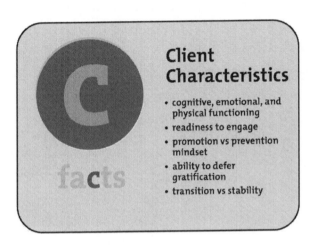

Client Characteristics

- cognitive, emotional, and physical functioning
- readiness to engage
- promotion vs prevention mindset
- ability to defer gratification
- transition vs stability

Consider what the next two case scenarios have in common.

Mark is a 36-year-old engineer, and the executor of his parents' very considerable estate. His parents died suddenly and unexpectedly while on holiday overseas. There are dozens of details for Mark to attend to in the midst of his grief. He and his four siblings are a fractious bunch; two of them are constantly calling and texting to demand their share of the inheritance. Mark's exasperated

*wife called me to set up an appointment for him after
watching Mark go berserk on their ten-year-old daughter
for leaving a towel on the bathroom floor.*

*Eleanor, age 58, is about to move in with a wonderful
new life partner. Both of them have been single for
several years after exiting unhappy marriages. They
joke that, having wallpapered and tiled their new home
together without committing gross acts of violence, they
know they are meant for each other. Eleanor's joy is being
muted somewhat by a flare-up of her lupus, the result of
forgetting to take her medication many times over the
past few months. Apparently, that isn't all she's forgotten:
Yesterday her partner fielded a call from the bank
inquiring about some long-overdue paperwork necessary
to approve their home renovation line of credit.*

Mark and Eleanor are in a time of considerable change.
Each of them is showing signs of running low on the personal
resources required to keep up with the new demands on them.
In his new role as an executor, Mark is facing a steep learning
curve and a greatly lengthened To Do list, all during a time
of intense mourning. His depletion is manifesting through a
decreased ability to manage his stress and to control his temper.
Eleanor's life changes are much happier ones, but she, too, is
facing an abnormally high number of decisions and additional
tasks. The tax on her cognitive bandwidth is showing up
through error-proneness and a neglect of everyday tasks and
self-care routines.

This combination of major life event and mental depletion is seen frequently in financial professionals' offices. In this chapter, we will examine why this is so, and what you can do about it.

Transitions pack a wallop

Both Mark and Eleanor are undergoing major life transitions, those big events that demarcate *what used to be* from *what is*.

I used to be married, but now I'm divorced.

I used to be struggling and anonymous, but now I'm rich and in the spotlight.

I used to be a corporate executive that everybody fawned over, but now I'm retired and largely overlooked.

Transitions can be anticipated or unexpected, welcomed or feared, voluntary or forced. They often involve fundamental shifts in self-identity and in social roles.

Sudden Money® Institute founder Susan Bradley teaches financial professionals that 'In a very direct way, transitions drive your business'. Clients reach out for financial guidance at a disproportionately high frequency when they are undergoing big life changes. If they get an inkling that the financial advisor who worked with the *Old Them* is not someone they can trust to work with the *New Them*, they may well look for a different advisor. This leads to a tremendous rate of firing of old advisors, and a correspondingly high rate of hiring new ones. Between 70% and 80% of the new clients in an advisor's practice, says Bradley, are people who are anticipating or have just gone through a major life event.[42]

Most transition events have significant financial implications, which is why clients ask for your guidance at such times. Yet it is entirely possible that they not be at their cognitive best for receiving and acting on that guidance. Like Mark, they can be grieving and beleaguered; like Eleanor, they can be tired and error-prone.

Non-adherence, then, can be the result of temporarily compromised neuropsychological functioning. Being in a major life transition increases the likelihood of that compromise, resulting in a state that I'll refer to as 'Transition Fatigue'. It shares some of the characteristics (described in Chapter 5) seen in people who have been dealing with scarcity, but tends to be longer-lasting and wider-reaching in terms of the associated mental depletion.

How mental energy comes and goes

Weighing in at just three pounds, your brain uses 20% of your resting metabolic calories. The organ is charged with everything from keeping your respiration going to decoding the underlying meaning of your colleague's tone of voice. Among the highest-order brain functions are those involved in acts of self-regulation, understood broadly as our ability to monitor, control and adapt our own thoughts, feelings, and behaviour in an ongoing, flexible manner.

The brain is constantly carrying out its own version of triage or air traffic control, activating and deactivating its assorted functions and processes behind the scenes, without conscious input or direction from you. The brain will always sacrifice non-critical functions for what it deems to be more important ones. Effortful acts of self-control and self-regulation are among the first to get placed on the altar.

Researchers from the fields of social psychology, behavioural economics and neuropsychology have done much to advance our knowledge in this area.* Studies indicate that mental energy is a finite but ever-renewing resource, akin to a reservoir of water. The reservoir is constantly being restored (through basic biological functions such as sleeping and eating), and is constantly being drawn from (through tasks of daily living). We all experience that ebb and flow on a daily basis. We've come to recognize our best times of day for getting work done as well as our slump times. We all know the experience of running out of energy before we run out of day; conversely, we all know the glorious, restorative effects of a nap and a bite to eat. Although sleep and food are the primary means of replenishing the reservoir, things like good habits, robust physical health, positivity, and strong social ties all help to maintain things in good working order, and even, ultimately, to increase the capacity of the reservoir.

An abrupt change of metaphor

You could also think of your mental energy as a pie, one that gets sliced up to support a number of different functions. The following chart – yup, it's a pie chart – is my representation of

---

* As I write this book, there is a particularly spirited debate going on in the world of psychology: Is mental energy truly as limited a resource as has been claimed? For purposes of this chapter, we will accept the commonsense notion that our mental capacity is, indeed, finite.

how our mental energy is used to fuel those aforementioned acts of self-regulation.

Where your mental energy goes...

Let's start with the top right sector and move clockwise through it.

1. **Managing pain and stress**: It takes energy to cope effectively. Stress is an experience of finding (or fearing) that the demands on you might exceed the resources you have to meet those demands. When we have experiences of physical pain or emotional suffering, we automatically reallocate some of our mental resources to address the problem. This can include actively seeking new solutions, reframing the problem, and

learning to persist in the face of pain that cannot be eliminated.

2. **Directing attention**: Part of the pie is taken up by the effort to sustain our focus and to resist distraction. I learned this firsthand as a student in an experimental school when I was a youngster. The building had no interior walls, which meant that students had to figure out early on how to focus their attention on *their* work, on *their* teacher, while simultaneously screening out noises from all the other classrooms. Directing attention took mental energy away from other important tasks – most notably, learning – with the result that the 'open concept' experiment failed miserably. As an adult, I find myself wondering how the teachers ever managed to cope with such chaos. (Come to think of it, maybe that's why so many of them smelled like weed.)

3. **Making decisions:** If you have ever organized a conference or planned a wedding, you will be aware of the phenomenon known as 'decision fatigue'. There comes a point where your brain starts to feel like the little spinning wheel of doom on the computer screen, churning away without making any discernible progress. That's the point at which you either decide to take a break (generally the best course of action) or press on and force yourself to continue making decisions even though you're depleted. It is my firm conviction that ugly bridesmaid dresses are the direct result of brides choosing the latter course.

4. **Resisting temptations:** Ever been on a diet? If so, you'll probably have experienced how quickly it all goes to

hell by the end of the day. It's not that you've lost the factual knowledge that apples are better for you than gummi bears. It's that you've run low on the very energy required to notice that you're getting 'tapped out', and are therefore more vulnerable to giving in to temptation.

5. **Controlling emotional displays:** One mark of maturity is that we generally do not melt down in public, throwing tantrums or sobbing uncontrollably like a two-year-old who has been denied a treat at the grocery store. While laudable, such acts of emotional restraint do tap into our reserves of mental energy.

6. **Forming new habits:** Without a doubt, well-established habits save you time and energy. They allow you to go on a kind of autopilot during your day, carrying out basic self-care, work, or household routines without needing to actively decide on each step along the way. But the process of *forming* a habit takes energy. Whether you're trying to get into the habit of eating more fibre, going to the gym, or keeping a gratitude journal, you will need to draw from your mental energy reservoir until the habit is established.

7. **Completing everyday chores:** Successful adulthood involves keeping up with the demands of household management. Making sure the bills are paid, the car has gas, the dishes are done, the children are picked up … this claims a good chunk of your energy. Recovering addicts are often surprised by how much energy is required, not just to resist temptation and stay sober, but to keep up with the tasks of daily life.

8. **Learning new things:** When was the last time you upgraded your computer's operating system, or switched to a new practice management software? You may have been surprised by just how taxing it can be to learn something new, particularly if it isn't inherently exciting or interesting. I frequently hear some variation of 'My brain hurts!' from clients who are having to decide between differing pension payouts or varying models of how to transfer a business to the next generation.

Help! I'm running out of pie!

What happens when life supersizes its demands? Unfortunately, you are not automatically handed a bigger pie; instead, you just have to carve up the existing pie differently. If you are experiencing a great deal of stress and turmoil in your family life, you may find that you're more distracted and that your housekeeping goes for a wholesale slide. If you have a new co-worker who is severely trying your patience, you will likely take a more generous slice of the pie for 'controlling emotional displays' or for 'resisting temptation' as you try not to throttle him or her; as a consequence of this reallocation of resources, you may well notice that you are diminished with respect to some of the other functions.

For the past several years, I have been working with the Financial Transitionist® Institute to study people who are in the midst of transitions such as career change, relocations, retirement, or divorce. Our preliminary research has found that major life transitions take a tremendous bite out of that mental energy pie. People whose transition events are long-lasting and predominantly negative (e.g. widowhood or a fractious divorce) are most susceptible to problematic levels of mental depletion. We are working right now to validate a Transition Fatigue questionnaire for financial professionals to use with their clients. Check the advisor side of my website at moneymindandmeaning.com for updates on the research, as well as for opportunities to use the questionnaire with your clients.

Mental depletion manifests differently for different people. There is not any single, dedicated neuropsychological indicator that screams 'Danger!'. But there are some telltale signs to be on the lookout for, both in your clients and yourself:

An intensification of emotion: This is the most reliable indicator that someone is running on empty. Emotions are heightened in both the positive and negative directions. Depleted people laugh more uproariously; they get irked more easily; they become tearful with less provocation. Normally reserved clients may be uncharacteristically emotional in your office. This indicator is often accompanied by the next sign.

Harder-to-control impulses: When people are depleted, it becomes harder for them not to act on strong emotions or momentary whims. This fatigue-induced degradation in self-control can be seen in neuroimaging studies. They show a reduction in the firing rate of neurons in various locales, including the anterior cingulate cortex. One of its functions is to detect discrepancies between what we are expecting or wanting to experience (e.g. a growing bank balance to fund a great vacation) and what we are actually experiencing (e.g. a free afternoon strolling around the outlet mall). As we lose the ability to detect such discrepancies ('Hey – saving money and going shopping really don't go together!'), we are more likely to act on the stronger or more pleasurable impulse. Regrettable actions are more likely to occur at such junctures.

Hunkering down: A very common yet maladaptive response to mental depletion is the tendency to withdraw from one's social network. While this may have the immediate effect of freeing up some time or reducing the need to put on the *everything-is-fine* face, it can be problematic in the long run. The research on this matter is unequivocal: The single best predictor of getting through stressful times, intact and thriving, is social support. Sometimes, of course, the problem is that the social support network is impoverished, or dysfunctional, or in some way just not up to the task of skilfully addressing a loved one's needs. This is often seen after transition events such as widowhood or divorce.

Decreased tolerance of stress and pain: When we're depleted, aches and pains seem to intensify, becoming harder to bear. Psychologists often make the distinction between *pain* versus *suffering* to explain this experience. The same number of physical pain 'units' can cause more pronounced suffering in someone whose reservoir has run dry. Similar decreases in tolerance can be found in the domain of coping with emotional pain. The same life stressors we've coped with before now seem more burdensome, resulting in increased fretfulness, sleep problems, pessimism, or difficulties relaxing.

Difficulty making decisions: Earlier, I mentioned the phenomenon of 'decision fatigue'. This usually manifests through increased dithering or equivocating. Some people, however, go to the other extreme and make decisions abruptly or capriciously, sometimes just to get them out of the way and over with. Advisors see both ends of the spectrum as they work with clients.

Widespread declines in routines requiring self-discipline: The exercise stops, the house is a disaster, and the inbox never gets cleared out. One of my patients described it thus: 'My *Give a Damn* button is busted.' Getting away from previously effective routines can lead to increased errors, such as missing appointments or failing to return promised documents.

Increased rigidity: Mental depletion is often manifested by an uncharacteristic unwillingness to compromise, be spontaneous, or go with the flow. Normally flexible people seem to morph into rigid control freaks. They simply do not have enough bandwidth to put up with anything that is not under their certain and direct control.

Size matters

My very proper mother and I shared a weakness for dessert and tea. One memorable day, we decided to visit a fancy teahouse we'd heard about. We were expecting linen tablecloths and fine china, and were not disappointed. We were a little taken aback, however, by the sullen waitress who seemed quite put out by the job requirement to actually serve people. We finally got her reluctant attention and placed our order. An eternity later, she brought our desserts to the table and barked out, 'Which one of youz ladies is the tart?' I was delighted to be able to indicate that my mother was, indeed, the tart.

I am often reminded of that question – 'Which one of youz is the tart?' – as I observe people's responses to setbacks in life. It is clear that not everyone is working with the same amount of mental energy. Some people operate with a Costco-sized version of the mental energy pie, and seem preternaturally gifted with high stress management capacities, remarkable self-restraint and self-discipline, and extraordinary adaptability. At the other end of the spectrum are the tarts (the small pastry kind of tart, not the hootchie-cootchie-momma kind). They can operate reasonably well within the scope of a low-demand, low-stress life, but they quickly show signs of strain. It doesn't take a major life transition to tap them out – a cat with an inconveniently timed hairball can do the trick.

What accounts for such differences? Given the profound biological underpinnings of mental energy, it is not surprising that genetics play a role. Individual differences in this regard are evident quite early in life, with some children consistently demonstrating higher levels of energy, along with a greater ability to recover their equanimity once they've had a snack and a nap. Genetics play a further role in various intellectual abilities. New learning, flexible problem solving, and organized planning simply come easier to some people than to others.

But biology is not destiny. It distresses me to admit that, throughout the 20th century, the field of psychology frequently promoted ideas of biological determinism. Among the tenets of the psychology gospel that have since been disproven are the following: 'Intelligence cannot be increased.' 'Stress kills.' 'You're either resilient or you're not.' 'Neural pathways are fixed by adolescence and cannot be altered.'

Wrong, every one of them.

Although genetics influence our energy levels and our outlook, they do not determine everything about them. In other words, we do not have to keep on being a tart! Some fixes for mental depletion are short term and relatively rapid – these have largely to do with restoring us to our usual levels. There are other approaches – ones with a longer timeframe – that work to increase the circumference of the pie and leave us with a greater capacity for self-regulation.

Money and struggle

Money plays an interesting role in all of this. Earlier in this book, I reviewed some of the recent studies on scarcity's effect on neuropsychological functioning. There is considerable evidence that financially straitened circumstances lead to mental depletion. I watched this happen recently to a dear artist friend, a brilliant man who lives a very lean lifestyle in order to make his art. A dental emergency landed him with a $200 bill that he could not readily absorb, and the stress response it generated led to some truly short-sighted decisions that caused further problems in his life. In your work as a financial professional, you have the ability to help such struggling people move into a financial safe zone, a place in which life's predictably unpredictable bills will not gravely destabilize or undo them.

People at the other end of the socioeconomic scale face different challenges in this regard. In his work with affluent families, Courtney Pullen cautions wealthy parents not to hamstring their children's development by protecting them from ever having to struggle. Pullen counsels parents to keep their protective impulses in check so as not to turn their kids' life journey into the kind of 'luxury excursion' that precludes the development of grit and resilience.[43]

An echoing sentiment is found in an adage credited to Oprah Winfrey: 'Where there is no struggle, there is no strength.' One sure way to thwart personal growth is to turn away from challenge and insist on remaining within a safe, familiar zone. Life transitions can come as a wake-up call, as an invitation to embrace the growth opportunities that show up on the journey from 'I used to be ...' into 'And now I'm ...'

Summary

We have a finite reserve of mental energy. While it usually renews itself daily, there are times when it cannot quite keep up with the demands of living. People undergoing major life transitions – particularly when those events are prolonged and negative – are especially vulnerable to such depletion. The risk of non-adherence is heightened in such worn-out clients.

Adherence Boosters

Whenever you have reason to suspect that a client may have become depleted, try one or more of these strategies:

1. Show them the pie chart on the last page of this book.* Explain that it represents how our mental energy gets used up in the course of a day. Tell them that you have been wondering how they're faring as they go through this period of life transition or challenge. Struggling clients will spontaneously point out the sectors where they're functioning sub-optimally. Ask them if they have noticed any of the key indicators of depletion discussed in the previous pages. These include stronger-than-usual emotions, reduced willpower, increased engagement in mindless activities, and social isolation or avoidance. You can also inquire if any of their family members or colleagues have voiced concerns about such things.

2. Remind them of the biological basis of their mental energy. Are they eating decently? How much sleep have they been getting? Have they been going out for walks or any form of physical activity? Many widowed clients report that

---

* Colour copies of the chart, printed on cardstock, can be ordered from the advisor side of my website at www.moneymindandmeaning.com. Clients really resonate with this image, and frequently request copies to take home with them.

they have not slept well in months. Others report they are getting by on tea and toast (or, worse yet, gin and tonic). Right then and there, some people will voice a commitment to addressing these problems. Ask if there is anything you can do to help them keep their resolution. Do they need the name of a family doctor, for example? Would they like a free pass for a visit to a gym? (This means, of course, that you need to have such things on hand.)

3. The primary adherence challenges with depleted clients are usually rooted in the fact that they (a) do not know where or how to begin tackling complex tasks, and (b) become easily overwhelmed. Be wary, therefore, about assigning any additional tasks to depleted clients – you do not want to contribute to their sense of being overwhelmed. Whenever you must give them things to do on their own, it is vital that you take them through the Readiness Questions (see Chapter 6) and determine how they will get things done.

4. Some clients may need to be reminded that their money could wisely be used to relieve some of their current burden. I have worked with many disciplined savers who seem to need permission to use funds to take their beleaguered spouse away on a holiday, or to pay for help in running the household when someone gets sick or when professional demands mount. Be aware that powerful money scripts are just as much at work in underspenders as in overspenders, and be prepared to help clients work through them.

5. Mentally depleted clients often complain that they have To Do lists that are a mile long. Part of the neuropsychological compromise for such clients can be an inability to differentiate high priority items from low priority ones. Your expertise can be called into action to help them ascertain what needs to be attended to immediately and what can wait until later (when their capacity has been restored). When clients leave your office with a well-organized, co-created action plan (Do this, then this, but hold off on that), it increases their sense of safety and confidence.

Whether they're mentally depleted or at the top of their game, all people do better when they have access to social support. In the next chapter, we look at how financial goal achievement is helped or hindered by other social and environmental influences (the 'S' in the FACTS model).

Chapter 8

Under the Influence:
Social and Environmental
Contributors to
Adherence

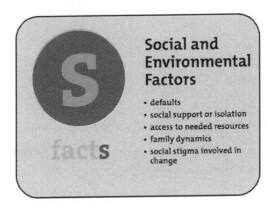

Social and Environmental Factors

- defaults
- social support or isolation
- access to needed resources
- family dynamics
- social stigma involved in change

facts

The late Dr. Chris Peterson was one of the most highly regarded scholars in positive psychology. He had a very succinct way of summarizing the entire canon of studies into human happiness. According to Peterson, it all boils down to this: *Other people matter.*

Support for that statement comes from the long-running Harvard Study of Adult Development, which began in 1938 with 268 Ivy League sophomores and continues to this day. Along the way, it was augmented by the wives and offspring of the original subjects, as well as by members of the broader Boston community. The purpose of the study? To uncover the secrets of successful aging. One of its most robust findings? That satisfying relationships are as close to an elixir of life as we have. Throughout the lifespan, secure social ties are among the strongest predictors of physical, cognitive and emotional well-being.

Interesting enough, but what, you may ask, does any of that have to do with financial adherence? Well, it turns out that *other people matter* with respect to how people behave around money. For example, you and your team matter hugely in this regard. Professional support and expertise help people take timely and sustained action, leading to better financial outcomes and overall well-being than are seen in those who try to do things on their own.

That's the good news. The more sobering news is that most financial professionals are just bit players compared to the other social influences on clients' financial lives. The best-laid plans can be scuttled by those *other people* within minutes of clients leaving your office. Here is a scenario shared with me by an advisor:

> *Andy is a widowed father of three daughters, now ranging in age from 15 to 21. The estate left to Andy by his wife four years ago was sufficient to allow all three girls to finish up their expensive private schools and to complete an undergraduate degree each – sufficient, that is, providing that Andy continued living roughly the*

same lifestyle as before her death, and that he invested the insurance money wisely. That, alas, was not the case. Very soon after his wife's death, Andy's expenses began to skyrocket. The beleaguered father told his concerned financial advisor that he was simply trying to make each of his daughters feel better during an intense period of grief. The advisor cautioned him repeatedly about the need to rein in his spending, but Andy voiced confidence that the financial hemorrhaging would stop once the girls got a little bit older and weren't missing their mum so much.

The day finally came when the principal had been reduced to the point where the tuition fees could no longer be covered. Andy and his advisor conferred for hours, finally devising a plan that would allow the youngest girl to finish up in the private high school as long as the oldest two took on student loans and part-time jobs to cover their own university tuition. Andy was equal parts regret and resolve as he left the office. Less than an hour later, however, he called back to report that the plan would not work. His oldest daughter had vehemently rejected the proposed plan, and was demanding that she be provided with a new car so that she could visit her out-of-state boyfriend more regularly. Could the advisor kindly release funds for the car?

There ought to be hazard pay for this work.

One of the challenges for financial professionals is to figure out who else has a say in the client's financial life. Kathleen Rehl is a researcher and an educator in the financial advising world. Early in her career as a CFP® professional, Rehl reports, she 'learned the hard way about the social stuff' – that is, about the reversals in the planning process that could be initiated by people outside the advising relationship. 'I'd meet with one spouse, who would go home and try to explain to their partner what we'd decided upon and why. They'd end up flustered or they'd lose confidence, and then we'd have to start all over again.' This gave birth to her policy of never taking on couples as clients unless both of them agreed to meet regularly during the crucial initial phase of planning. Rehl credits this policy with saving time and frustration all around. It paid further dividends down the road, equipping her to provide highly attuned support and direction to the surviving spouse when the other party died. [44]

While spouses and children are obvious sources of influence on your clients, there are bound to be others. Business associates, religious leaders, friends, that guy on the television – they all weigh in with considerable regularity. Some may simply be reminding your clients of unyielding financial commitments ('You need to be reinvesting 3% of your profits back into the business.'), whereas others may be voicing strongly biased opinions ('You're stupid if you pay some lawyer to write up a will when you can just do it yourself.') It's a good idea to find out whose ideas hold sway in your clients' lives. *Other people matter.*

Identifying the unhelpful influences

At times, clients may be acting under the influence of long-ago people in their lives. Those influences have contributed to the unconscious money scripts (described in Chapter 4) that are in operation to this day. Clients may not know who or what is driving their actions.

But many clients know full well who is contributing to the problems they are trying to address. Even as you assure them that they can spend more money and enjoy the fruits of their labour, they may be wincing in anticipation of judgmental responses from their tightwad parents. Or even as they head out the door with a few solid investment options to choose from, they may know that their braggart golf buddy is going to make them feel like a chump as he crows about his latest triumphs in day trading.

Complicating this issue is the fact that talking about money matters doesn't come easily to most people. In Kathleen Rehl's current work of training other financial professionals, she emphasizes the double-barrelled need to *insist* that clients have 'money conversations' with the key people in their life, and then to *support* them in doing so. Such talks are often emotionally fraught – e.g. sharing estate planning decisions with adult children, or having candid conversations about net worth and financial values with potential life partners. When clients balk at dealing with potential pushback from loved ones, advisors should offer to help facilitate the conversations. Rehl cautions, 'You can't just hope it goes away.'

The alternative to avoidance and denial is to ask, directly, whether clients expect to encounter opposition to the proposed plan of action. Reviewing likely objections to your advice isn't just about bolstering a client's ability to stay the course in the face of opposition. It's a valuable exercise in and of itself for what it reveals to you about the client's life and formative influences.

If you can force yourself to remain open to the shocking possibility that you can be wrong, on occasion, then this exercise offers further value in helping you uncover your own blind spots and biases. Looking at your advice from a naysayer's perspective is a great way of acknowledging that you, too, have a human brain that is vulnerable to sloppy thinking. Most readers of this book will have had exposure to teachings about the cognitive biases and heuristics that can hamper good decisions: things such as confirmation bias, availability heuristic, spotlight effect, anecdotal fallacy, attribution error, etc. The naysayers in your clients' lives can help expose and check some of these biases and faulty assumptions. The willingness to engage in an open-minded review of objections is a hallmark of a great advisor.

Finding the helpful influences

One of my first mentors in the field of financial change was Barbara Stanny, the author of several bestselling books that explore the beliefs undergirding earning, spending, saving, investing and philanthropy.[45] Stanny's books contain powerful messages about the need for individuals to do the 'inner work' of money so that they can go out and do the 'outer work' of financially successful behaviour. Notwithstanding her belief in the power of the individual, Stanny is quick to dash the myth of individualism. Her assertion is that no one can escape from financial instability without guidance, input, and encouragement from other people.

Her strong belief in this regard was formed over the course of conducting hundreds of research interviews. Stanny found that there was a strong differentiator between struggling women who went on to achieve financial stability versus those who remained in financial chaos, no matter their level of earnings. That differentiator was the extensive support network that surrounded the former group versus the relative isolation of the latter. *All* of the former, she discovered, had folks in their lives who each offered their own brand of support to aid them in their quest for financial clarity, higher earnings, and investing success. Some cheered them on and celebrated progress; some listened to their innermost doubts and yearnings; some provided glowing examples of how to do things right; and still others delivered helpful information or facilitated connections. Those who changed for the better were able to use that support to make personal and professional breakthroughs. In light of those findings, Stanny became a firm believer in the need for people to find their voice and ask for what they want or need in order to make financial progress.

Support comes in different flavours

Social science research bears out Stanny's conclusions. Humans need different kinds of social support to reach their potential and to be buffered from the inevitable hard knocks of life. Among the most commonly researched forms of support are the following:

1. *Emotional support* – demonstrations or expressions of empathy, love, loyalty, etc.

2. *Informational support* – the delivery of useful guidance and advice.

3. *Instrumental* (or *tangible*) *support* – the provision of material goods or services.

4. *Companionship* – the carrying out of shared activities.

All forms of support have a role to play in well-being. Imagine, for example, that you have a child who is in the hospital. You might benefit from the *emotional support* offered by your best friend during a late-night phone call, from the *informational support* offered by a staff member on where to find affordable parking, from the *tangible support* that arrives in the form of hot meals delivered to your home by a thoughtful group of neighbours, and from the *companionship* of a family member who quietly shares the bedside vigil with you.

Most financial professionals excel at providing informational support. The best among you view yourselves as adherence partners, and make a point of sending your clients supportive tips, regular reminders, and encouraging updates on how they're progressing with respect to their goals. Many of you also offer additional emotional support by virtue of your deep listening skills, warmth, and encouragement. Even so, you are just a small part of the circle of influence on your clients' lives. You can greatly extend your sphere of support by introducing clients to other helpful people, organizations and sources of ongoing inspiration and guidance. This personnel expansion restores and builds clients' capacity, so that they can carry out the recommendations they agreed upon with you.

In my experience, very few financial professionals are aware of the fantastic value that exists in their contact list. Your connections in the community allow you to make timely referrals for clients needing help that you cannot provide. They may need a therapist, a mentor or a support group if they are going to be able to get through hard times, intact, and to persist in attaining their goals (whether that goal is making it through an onerous debt repayment plan or expanding a successful business). New resources are especially needed when the client's existing social influences are unhelpful or inadequate to meet their current needs.

Anytime you are working with a client undergoing a major life transition, you should be vigilant to the possibility that they may need additional supports. Transition events bring about profound changes in clients' self-identity; when such changes occur, their existing networks may not be up to the task of supporting them as usual. Lottery winners are often stunned by the ways their friendships change post-windfall. Widows and widowers usually isolate themselves in their grief for extended periods, re-emerging only to find that they feel out of place with friends who are still part of a couple. First-generation wealth builders may feel shocked and dismayed by their children's infighting over the business transfer, but have no idea who to turn to for help and support.

This is where you can shine. You can provide names of specialists in the related fields. You can offer to facilitate a first meeting. You can send them a book written just for their situation. By expanding their access to informational, instrumental, emotional, or companionship supports, you let clients know that you are one of their best resources.

An unexpected source of Adherence Boosters can be those longstanding clients who refer their friends to you. Kathleen Rehl has experienced this directly and observed it in other advisors working with widows. Beyond making the initial introduction, longstanding clients often lovingly 'nagged' their friends to complete important tasks: 'Did you get the paperwork back to Kathleen yet?' 'Have you finished that exercise she gave you?' 'Do you want me to take you to that government office so you can finish up the application?' Such is the value of social support.

Broaden the view

Thus far, we have only been considering ways in which certain individuals in our clients' lives can boost or detract from adherence. This is too narrow a view. Cultural and environmental factors – religious, linguistic, regional, organizational – can exert powerful influences on financial values and subsequent behaviour. Faced with clients who are slamming the brakes on widely accepted advice, a naïve advisor may falsely conclude that a client has personal 'issues' with money, issues that somehow need to be ferreted out and removed so that good practices can be adopted. But these beliefs or practices may be rooted in deeply inculcated cultural values that are different from the advisor's own.

Here in Central Canada, for example, most indigenous peoples are raised with the ethic that their personal resources are to be shared freely with the extended family and wider community. Clients who come from this background have reported to me that they find it distressing to build up retirement savings when so many of the people they love are struggling to meet basic current needs. The majority of my Mennonite clients place a high value on peaceful and simple living, and steadfastly resist both lifestyle creep and opportunities to invest in companies with any ties to the military. Many of my Muslim clients refuse to put money into interest-bearing bank accounts, and are manifestly uncomfortable with standard practices in personal investing. I know people from all three of these backgrounds who have been condemned by financial professionals for holding values that are – and I quote directly – 'illogical', 'stupid', and 'unworkable'. That is just breathtakingly arrogant.

It is not our job as financial professionals to determine the rightness or rationality of a client's world view, or to weigh in on which cultural values should be honoured and which should be rejected. Rather, it is our task to hold skilful conversations with all clients in order to help them (1) clarify their values, and (2) determine how best to meld those values with their goals, with available opportunities, and with regulatory and actuarial realities. Over the course of decades spent working as an accountant and CFP® professional, Denver-based Jim Williams has learned the importance of coming into alignment with clients' felt needs and aspirations, even when those things might lead them down a path that is not actuarially optimal. 'It is our duty as advisors to honour *their* desires, and to do our best to help them fulfil those. Oh – and to document, document, document!'[46]

Dr. Rehman Abdulrehman is a psychologist who consults to industry and government on cultural diversity and the overcoming of bias.[47] He teaches that the starting point for effective cross-cultural conversations is coming to understand our *own* world view. Without such self-awareness, our unconscious biases can become strong drivers of our decision-making and interactions. Such biases can lead to inadvertent acts of 'micro-aggressions', those subtle but externally observable behaviours that indicate we think less of a client because of differing values or practices. The very least that our clients can do in response is to not take our advice, not continue the relationship, and not refer others to us.

On the plus side, Dr. Abdulrehman claims that opportunities abound for organizations and teams that welcome employees, customers, and suppliers with differing world views. The financial services industry has begun to get on board this opportunity train. Witness, for example, the mutual fund options that exist for those not wanting to invest in weapons manufacturers or environmentally harmful industries. Other institutions are stepping up to offer non-interest-bearing bank accounts. Such initiatives demonstrate that cultural differences are not a nuisance. They offer significant growth possibilities for those willing to embrace them.

A nudge or a shove?

With each year that passes, I have become increasingly respectful of the power of our physical and social environment to shape our choices – both for good *and* for ill. Marshall Goldsmith has described the environment as a 'nonstop triggering mechanism whose impact on our behavior is too significant to be ignored'.[48] And yet we often *do* ignore it, relying on willpower and motivation and memory to pull us through when what we really need are systems, habits, reminders, helpful defaults, and strategic avoidance.

One need only consider the consumer culture in which we all live and breathe to note how significantly financial behaviour is shaped by external forces. There is a billion-dollar advertising industry that exists solely to make people part with their money. It is remarkably successful in making them feel inadequate, and in both shoving and nudging them to purchase products and experiences.

There are times when circumstances warrant the imposition of stringent environmental controls in order to limit financially undesirable influences. In Washington, D.C. several years ago, personnel from the National Football League (NFL) Players' Association found themselves in just such a position.

> We had to institute a policy of 'No Cell Phones During Meetings'. Too many of the players were getting the touch put on them by friends and family members, right in the middle of team meetings when crucial information about game strategy was being outlined. 'Why'd you give your sister a better car than you gave me?' 'When are you going to buy me a bigger house?' Guys were getting completely stressed out and distracted by it all, so we made it a rule that they had to put away their personal phones for a few hours.[49]

Although it was only a narrow solution to a much broader problem in the players' lives, the rule worked perfectly to stop a problematic behaviour at a critical time.

Most financial professionals cannot impose such ironclad policies or rules on clients. Sometimes, however, clients will agree to voluntarily submit themselves to an external rule for the sake of their financial well-being. An example of this includes the establishment of *a priori* profit and loss guidelines that will automatically trigger the selling and buying of investments. Clients' pre-commitment to these guidelines replaces their fear-based or excitement-based decisions with policy-driven ones that they co-create with you.

There's the rub!

Behavioural economists often use the word 'friction' when describing the inherent tendency of a procedure or system to slow down progress. Such hindrances are relatively small stones on the path to task completion. Friction is often contrasted with dauntingly massive barriers (poverty, racism, etc.) that are much harder to address. Even though the impediments caused by friction may be relatively small, their impact is not. 'Every click, step, field, form and signature is just as significant as a large-scale barrier,' according to the behavioural economics experts at Common Cents Lab.[50] For example, if you send new clients a form to sign and return as a condition of bringing them into your practice, you have just introduced some friction into the client engagement process. As a result, the paperwork may not get done in as timely a manner as you might wish – or, indeed, it might not get done at all.

For proof of the power of friction, one need look no further than the data on organ donation rates. Countries requiring people to *opt in* to having their organs harvested automatically after death have much lower rates of donation than countries who require people to *opt out*. This is really quite remarkable, when you think of it: The only action required either to opt in or opt out is the simple act of checking a box. People hate the active decision-making involved in checking the box, with the result that the default option reigns supreme. (Just how lazy *is* humanity, anyway?!)

The challenge for you and your team is to figure out how to *remove* friction that works to a client's disadvantage, and how to *add* it in when that would be beneficial. Providing self-addressed stamped envelopes for clients is a commonly adopted strategy for removing unhelpful friction. On the flip side, positive psychology expert Shawn Achor is a big proponent of adding helpful friction. He claims that, by putting 20 seconds' worth of obstacles or inconveniences between ourselves and the thing that we shouldn't be doing (e.g. obsessively checking stock market performance, or mindlessly eating, or reflexively reaching for the remote control), we become far less likely to carry out that undesirable behaviour.[51] Twenty seconds can be all that is needed for many of us to move beyond our immediate impulses and to get in touch with our better intentions. This is the rationale behind such commonplace recommendations as having spendthrifts freeze their credit cards in a bucket of water, or in turning off 1-click ordering options. In the words of willpower experts Roy Baumeister and John Tierney, 'Vice delayed is often vice denied.'[52]

Be careful what you draw attention to

This past tax season, I was asked to do a television interview about a recently released report on tax-filing procrastination. This came on the heels of similar requests for interviews about other alarmist press releases relating to personal finance – mounting consumer debt levels, for example, or the growing number of failure-to-launch college graduates. In the past, I might have been inclined to jump right onto Chicken Little's bandwagon and decry the growing number of people making bad financial decisions.

But that was before I was hit by the wand of the 'Social Proof Fairy', aka Robert Cialdini. Social proof is a commonly used heuristic or cognitive shortcut that humans engage in when trying to figure out the best course of action. It involves looking at other people's choices in order to determine what we should be doing, choosing, or believing. Social proof is linked to such disparate things as participation in recycling initiatives, appraisals of whether something is funny or worthwhile, and the desirability of consumer products. It explains the power of Oprah's Book Club and the addictive nature of Likes on Facebook.

Cialdini's research has shown that drawing attention to bad behaviour can backfire, and inadvertently increase the propensity of others to engage in it. For example, when Cialdini first endeavoured to help stop the theft of rocks by visitors to Arizona's National Petrified Forest, he noted that the posted signs read, 'Your heritage is being vandalized every day by theft losses of petrified wood of 14 tons a year, mostly a small piece at a time.' He was concerned that this was sending precisely the wrong message: namely, that petty thieving had become commonplace, or even normative. Subsequent experimentation with the signage indicated that it was better to have no signage at all than to post messages that implied theft was a widespread and growing problem.

The alternative to highlighting the growing rates of bad behaviour, argues Cialdini, is to provide social proof that the majority of people do the *right* thing. For example, he helped the British government improve their collection rate on outstanding taxes from 57% to 87%. His intervention? Adding just a single sentence to the collection letter: 'Most people pay their taxes on time.' Cialdini reports that the best social proof initiatives tap into three basic motivations at the same time: to make decisions easily, to feel good about oneself, and to fit in with others.[53]

Whether participating in media interviews or working directly with my financial therapy clients, I endeavour to use social proof to nudge people towards effective action. I talk about the fact that the majority of citizens file their taxes on time, and pay off their credit cards in full every month. I reserve the more negatively tinged information for drawing attention to the downsides of the bad choice – the stress of mounting bills, for example, or the increase in marital conflicts in families with unaddressed debt problems. But I always return to the good habits that support financial stability, and provide concrete recommendations for how to get on the Bound-for-Glory train.*

Summary

No one does well without social support. You and your team are important sources of support, yourselves, and can provide

---

* This practice extends to my personal life, too. Over time, beloved youngsters in my life have received gems of social proof ranging from 'Winnie the Pooh and Tigger go to bed on time' all the way up to 'The majority of teenagers do not have sex while in high school.' The first was highly effective. Check in with me later regarding the second.

additional recommendations and referrals that are of help to clients with impoverished networks or greatly changed personal circumstances. Cultural and environmental factors also exert strong influences on financial values and decisions. It is important to understand the external drivers of your clients' behaviour so that you can help bolster the helpful ones and mitigate the unhelpful ones.

Adherence Boosters

1. As you well know from previous chapters, the ideal way of dealing with non-adherence is to anticipate it *before* it messes with the agreed-upon plan. This holds true for non-adherence related to social factors. Familiarize yourself with the following questions, and make a point of asking them regularly:

   - Is there anyone in your life who might be upset by this plan?
   - How would you like to handle that?
   - Do you feel ready to have conversations with these people on your own?
   - How might we help to create realistic expectations about what you are and aren't willing to do?
   - What might the plan look like if the people upset by it were right? How would we know if we were wrong about this plan?

2. Offer to help clients have respectful, assertive conversations. Give them opportunities to practise their responses in

front of you. Where appropriate, you can also offer to facilitate such conversations, or to meet with concerned family members on your own. Just make sure that you are not setting yourself up for one of those fools-rush-in-where-angels-fear-to-tread situations. Get written consent that outlines what you are/are not allowed to disclose. And consider whether such a meeting needs to be handled by a different kind of professional: a family business consultant, for example, or a mediator.

3. When clients predict that they will encounter great resistance in carrying out their desired course of action, offer to be the fall guy for them. This is especially helpful for clients who keep capitulating to others' relentless demands for handouts. Andy, the widowed father of three who was discussed in the first part of this chapter, could well have benefited from such a strategy: 'My financial planner has told me that I can't buy you *or* me a car. The money has been put away for tuition, and I can't get at it for any other purpose.'

4. Discover and harness the client's positive social influences wherever possible. The following questions can help boost confidence and persistence:

    • Who has been a role model for you in regards to how they live their life?
    • Who has taught you valuable lessons about money? What do you admire about how they've worked? How they've given to others? How they've dealt with their finances?

- Who in your life will be the most excited about what you're trying to do?
- Is there anyone you'd like to reach out to for help in reaching your goals? What would you like them to know about your goals and how you're going to achieve them?

5. Your contact list is one of the most important resources you have to offer your clients who need extra support or specialized services. Your list of pre-vetted attorneys, therapists, accountants, trustees, money coaches, marriage counsellors, etc. is tremendously valuable. It saves clients time and worry about how they might possibly assess the ethics and competence of strangers that show up on a Google search. It is important that you avoid any conflicts of interest in making these referrals. Where possible, offer two or three names of people you think would be suitable.

6. When you do make a referral or recommendation, follow up on it! Even the best practitioner in the area may not be a good fit for every one of your potential referrals to him or her. Moreover, people can and do change over time with respect to such things as their preferred area of practice, the quality of their service delivery, and even their ethical conduct. Make a point of checking in with your clients:

- Did they make an appointment?
- Did they attend?
- Are there any concerns?
- What is the plan for moving forward?

7. When it comes time to expand your team, consider hiring people who bring different perspectives to the table. Monoculture is just as problematic in financial offices as it is in horticulture. A mix of ages, genders, and ethnic and religious backgrounds equips you to serve a broader array of clients with the sensitivity and skill they deserve. (As an added bonus, your office potlucks improve immeasurably.)

8. Use social proof to draw attention to desirable behaviour and to provide hope:

    'The vast majority of our team's clients reach their retirement goals.'

    'A lot of clients benefit from this exercise.'

    'Many others have been through debt repayment programmes and still have been able to buy their own house someday. You can do it, too.'

Some Final Thoughts

Good advice of any kind can be hard to take; good financial advice, particularly so. That's part of what makes it so rewarding and frustrating, so heartbreaking and satisfying, to work with people and their money. In this book, we have focused on how to get better at giving *advice that sticks* – that is, advice that gets implemented in a timely manner to accomplish its intended purpose.

To be clear, following the recommendations in this book does not ensure that you will be able to sidestep all future adherence challenges. You will continue to encounter people who struggle mightily with deciding on a course of action, initiating the necessary steps, and persisting until the job is done. What has changed is that you now have the knowledge and related processes to address those adherence dilemmas. When you combine that knowledge with a willingness to handle implementation impasses, you will start to have a different experience of your work. You will have less exasperation and more curiosity; less judgment and more compassion; less pessimism and more success.

Dozens of adherence-boosting strategies and recommended questions were covered in the previous chapters. If pressed to nominate the best strategies for a motivated practitioner to start with, I would suggest the following:

1. At the outset of each meeting (or beforehand, if possible), ask: 'What will make this meeting the best possible use of your time, energy and money?' Organize the meeting accordingly. (Chapter 2)
2. Develop the gift of presence: listen attentively; speak plainly; connect warmly. (Chapter 3)
3. Use the three Readiness Questions to ensure you have established a mutually agreed-upon plan that is meaningful and manageable. (Chapter 6)

These strategies are part of a disciplined, evidence-based process that will enhance your effectiveness as an advice-giver. They will help you and your clients to bridge the gap between intention and action.

Even so, there will still be problems. In these next few pages, I will address some remaining challenges that I frequently come across in my own clinical work and consultation practice. I hope the proposed solutions or approaches will be of interest and use to you.

Where it usually falls apart

I am frequently asked to consult on cases where the desired action or behaviour change is not happening. The individual client details vary tremendously in terms of such things as net worth, level of education, and access to other resources.

Overwhelmingly, however, these non-compliant clients have one thing in common: Most have never fully agreed to the plan put forward by the financial professional. The advice-givers have simply assumed readiness on the part of the client, ignoring or glossing over evidence that the client is not prepared to engage in the proposed plan. Let's review the purpose of the three Readiness Questions, and consider the implications of neglecting them.

Readiness Question 1: 'How would you feel about (insert recommended action here)?'

This is your time to explore whether you're focusing on the thing that the client most wants to engage in, and whether you have mutual agreement on what to do next. If the response is lukewarm, or worse, pay attention to that! Ignoring the client's half-heartedness means that you are likely to be off-target in whatever else you propose or expect.

Readiness Question 2: 'If you decided to (insert recommended action here), how would that benefit you?'

This is your chance to determine that the client has an emotional connection to the plan, one that is sufficiently deep to help him or her persist through future periods of discouragement or temptation or competing demands. Again, if the client's response indicates only a vague or intellectual assent to the proposed action, then there may be insufficient motivation for moving ahead with your plan. Ignoring this fact is akin to *pretending* that you have an emotionally engaged client. It would be kind of adorable if it weren't so futile.

Readiness Question 3: 'If you decided to go ahead with this step, how confident are you that you could do it?'

This is one of your best opportunities to boost the client's sense of self-efficacy, as well as to address foreseeable barriers to their progress. Skipping this step leaves the client vulnerable to being torpedoed by events that were preventable or addressable. However unfairly, such setbacks or outright failures become associated in their minds with *you*. Avoidance of, and dissatisfaction with, your services often increase as a result.

Yup – it slows you down, but then it speeds things up

I suspect that you, like me, often feel pressed for time in client meetings. If that is the case, then you may well be tempted to jettison some of the steps above like they were so much unnecessary ballast. I understand that impulse, and can promise that you can, indeed, get away with skipping some of those steps, at least some of the time. I can also assure you that it is the skipped steps that are most likely to trip you up.

When you commit to giving advice that has a better chance of 'sticking', it adds a few minutes to your initial client meetings. Adding time to save time can make you feel inefficient – kind of like spending money to save money, as my car mechanic so cheerfully tells me whenever I grumble about bringing in the car for routine maintenance – but the fact is that it does, indeed, save time in the long run. It also prevents wasted efforts, preserves positive relationships, and makes everybody happier with the end result. Advisors tell me it also leads to more referrals from very satisfied clients.

The glorious relief of stating the obvious

The previous strategies notwithstanding, there will be times when the mutually agreed-upon action plan has come to a full and complete stop. You send out reminder notices, leave cheerful or no-nonsense voicemail messages, camp out on their front lawn, and eventually secure a promise for a prompt response ... which continues to not happen. What is the right response to an implementation standstill?

I believe that bringing the impasse out into the open is the best option. Doing so breathes new life into a relationship or an action plan that has grown stagnant. Your own personality strengths such as curiosity, humility, and openness can be utilized to great effect in such moments. The following are sample inquiries that advice-givers in my consultation practice have found useful:

> From my point of view, things seem to have ground to a halt. Does it feel to you that there hasn't been a lot of change or movement? If this keeps on, I'm concerned you're going to stop coming here altogether. Could we talk about what's going on?

Such an inquiry is non-defensive, non-attacking, and inviting. Clients often are visibly relieved when the reality of their stuck-ness is acknowledged in such a way.

Here's another approach:

> I'm concerned I'm not being of much service to you. We haven't been able to make much headway on the problems you hired me to solve, and I'm sorry about that.

*Is there something we could do differently in order to get
things moving in the right direction?*

Notice the apology that is part of this invitation to discuss
the problem. You may be tempted to write it off as one of those
stereotypically Canadian quirks of apologizing for everything,
but it is not, in fact, a gratuitous apology. Neither is it an
assumption of blame. Rather, it is a sincere expression of regret
for the impasse. This non-defensive approach broadcasts your
willingness to change things up at your end, if that's what needs
to happen. (NB: You need to actually *be* willing to change things
up at your end, if that's what needs to happen; otherwise, don't
offer to do so.)

I wonder as you wander

Then there's the wonderful world of opportunities offered by
'I'm wondering …' statements:

> *I'm wondering if …*   *we're dealing with the right issue.*
> *we're starting with the right task.*
> *this is the right approach.*
> *this is the right time.*

It is important to check in with people regarding changes
to their life circumstances. Perhaps something has occurred
that has introduced competing demands, chewing up a
significant portion of their mental energy 'pie' (see Chapter 7)
and rendering your initial plan too ambitious for their current
capacity. An agile advisor will adapt the plan to meet the client's
current capability.

'I'm wondering ...' statements can be used to raise the possibility that even more significant changes might be needed to the advising relationship, itself:

I'm wondering if you need a different kind of help than I can provide.

I'm wondering whether we should think about bringing somebody else on board to help us out.

This can be your opportunity to make referrals to people from other professions, including psychologists, lawyers, family business consultants, etc.

Not every dog is the right dog

Visit any bookstore with a section on pets, and you are apt to come across titles such as *The Right Dog for You* or *Choosing the Perfect Puppy*. The books are premised on the notion that some breeds of dog will be a better fit for your lifestyle and personality than others. A greyhound makes a better running companion than a basset hound; a Doberman makes a better guard dog than a golden retriever.

Persistent adherence challenges with a particular client (or type of client) should raise the possibility that this is not the right dog for you. Indicators that you may need to transfer, refer or even fire the client include frank rudeness towards you and your staff, frequent miscommunications, and unreasonable demands for your time and attention. Then there are the indicators that come from your own physical or emotional reactions to the client. Symptoms such as persistent dread, sleeplessness, or anxiety are not just inconveniences; rather, they are clarion calls to address the fact that this client is taking a toll on your well-being.[54]

There will be times when you really do not want to lose the business of a difficult client, or when you simply do not have the authority to fire him or her (e.g. you are an employee of a bank rather than the owner of a private firm). In these cases, you should try to divvy up the contact with other team members, or transfer that client to a co-worker.

Remember this: You don't need to keep going at this alone. Coaching or supervision can be useful in such situations. There may be particular skills you need to develop (e.g. assertiveness or flexibility); there may be new perspectives on the problem. When you avail yourself of one or more of the various kinds of social support outlined in Chapter 8, professional and personal breakthroughs become more likely.

There may well come a time, however, when the only sensible and ethical thing to do is to refer a troublesome client elsewhere. Persistent adherence challenges are among the tip-offs that it is time to say goodbye. On those occasions when you do need to fire someone from your practice, do your best to keep the terminations respectful and cordial. Avoid adding a layer of shame or sense of failure to either the client or yourself.

People in metal houses shouldn't throw live wires

Earlier in this book, I compared money to a Van de Graaff generator, explaining that, for many people, money carries a powerful emotional charge. This charge can thwart their ability to make sound financial decisions and to carry out the actions required to meet their goals. Much good advice has been burned to a crisp by clients' conflicted emotions and beliefs about money (and the unskilled handling of them).

You are more likely to get zapped in your line of work if you have not done any examination of your own relationship to money. Such an examination involves coming to understand how you've come to believe and behave as you do regarding all aspects of your financial life: giving, saving, earning, investing, competing, retiring, growing, simplifying, disclosing, compromising, etc.

One can be an absolute genius with respect to the outer (or technical) side of money and still be clueless about dealing with the inner aspects. How else to explain what my clients tell me they have encountered in the offices of financial professionals? A discouraged, unemployed young graduate was forced to endure a shame-filled, high-volume lecture from a banker when he missed a student loan payment. Bereaved parents were repeatedly told by a structured settlement expert how lucky they were to be the recipients of a wrongful death payout. A retired couple wanting to distribute their wealth to charity were begged by a tearful advisor to not reduce the size of their account with her.

As these examples illustrate, your own financial values and beliefs have the power to generate strong emotions that can interfere with skilled and ethical advising. This occurs most reliably when some event or person violates a core assumption you hold regarding how things *should* be, or when something gets in the way of your own ambitions or ego. It is helpful to spend time reflecting on the drivers of your own financial behaviours and broader outlook on life. It is important that you learn to identify the signs that you've been zapped, and what to do in response.

You can change most anything or nothing at all

If the last 20 years of social science and neuroscience have taught us anything, it's this: Pretty much every human quality or skill can be improved through the sustained application of effort. 'Growth mindset' is the term applied by psychologists to describe the awareness and conviction that you can get better at the things that matter to you.[55] The growth mindset is associated with an astonishing array of positive outcomes, including mental, physical, relational, and financial well-being. Each of us needs to discern whether it's worth the effort to learn a different way of being and doing – and, of course, we need to get the kind of *advice that sticks* that will support us in sustaining those changes.

Fortunately, there are now more opportunities than ever for you to develop expertise with the personal side of your work. There are in-depth certification programmes that focus on interpersonal skills such as deep listening and the conveyance of warmth. There are specialty training tracks that equip you to meet the needs of a particular niche or demographic. There are networks of financial professionals who gather for collaboration and support in making those changes. There are also many fine coaches and therapists who specialize in the interior aspects of this work – helping you develop personal insight and learn skills in self-management – so that you can show up as a healthier, happier, more helpful human being.

Consider this a call for you to become part of an emerging new guild of financial professionals, a guild made up of people who are fully equipped to address the needs, the opportunities, and the gifts inherent in working with people and their finances. You are being invited to experience what Frederick Buechner was thinking of when he wrote of the highest level of vocation, that place 'where your deep gladness and the world's deep hunger meet.'[56]

I hope our paths cross soon in that place.

Recommended Reading

The books in this section were selected with two things in mind: usefulness and enjoyment. I found each of them to be thought-provoking, a pleasure to read, and highly applicable. I hope that you, too, will find some gems in here.

Because I am constantly coming across compelling new writers and materials, it made sense to create an online version of this section that could be updated as needed. Visit it anytime at www.advicethatsticks.com. There is no registration or sign-up needed. This is where I have included additional links to fantastic blogs and great training opportunities. Feel free to drop me a line and make suggestions for new materials to add to the list.

Personal reflections on money:

Money, a Memoir: Women, Emotions and Cash (2006) by Liz Perle. Picador.

Lost and Found: One Woman's Story of Losing Her Money and Finding her Life (2011) by Geneen Roth. Viking.

Sacred Success: A Course in Financial Miracles (2014) by Barbara Stanny. BenBella.

The Thin Green Line: The Money Secrets of the Super Wealthy (2015) by Paul Sullivan. Simon and Schuster.

Broader explorations of money:

> *Dollars and Sense: How We Misthink Money and How to Spend Smarter* (2017) by Dan Ariely. Harper.

> *Happy Money: The Science of Happier Spending* (2014) by Elizabeth Dunn and Michael Norton. Simon and Schuster.

> *Conscious Finance: Uncover Your Hidden Money Beliefs and Transform the Role of Money in Your Life* (2007) by Rick Kahler and Kathleen Fox. FoxCraft.

> *Mind Over Money: The Psychology of Money and How to Use It Better* (2016) by Claudia Hammond. Anansi.

> *Financial Recovery: Developing a Healthy Relationship with Money* (2011) by Karen McCall. New World.

> *Scarcity: Why Having Too Little Means So Much* (2013) by Sendhil Mullainathan and Eldar Shafir. Times Books.

> *Financial Planning 3.0: Evolving Our Relationships with Money* (2016) by Richard Wagner. Outskirts Press.

Resources on decision-making:

> *Predictably Irrational: The Hidden Forces that Shape Our Decisions* (2009) by Dan Ariely. Harper.

> *Payoff: The Hidden Logic That Shapes Our Motivation* (2016) by Dan Ariely. TED Books.

Sudden Money: Managing a Financial Windfall (2000) by Susan Bradley and Mary Martin. Wiley.

The Wisest One in the Room: How to Harness Psychology's Most Powerful Insights (2017) by Thomas Gilovich and Lee Ross. Free Press.

Decisive: How to Make Better Choices in Life and Work (2013) by Chip Heath and Dan Heath. Random House.

Willful Blindness: Why We Ignore the Obvious at Our Peril (2011) by Margaret Heffernan. Anchor Random House.

Thinking, Fast and Slow (2013) by Daniel Kahneman. Anchor Random House.

Further ideas about facilitating change:

Willpower: Rediscovering the Greatest Human Strength (2011) by Roy Baumeister and John Tierney. Penguin.

Pre-Suasion: A Revolutionary Way to Influence and Persuade (2016) by Robert Cialdini. Simon and Schuster.

Smarter Faster Better: The Secrets of Being Productive (2017) by Charles Duhigg. Penguin Random House.

Switch: How to Change Things When Change is Hard (2010) by Chip Heath and Dan Heath. Random House.

Facilitating Financial Health: Tools for Financial Planners, Coaches, and Therapists (2008) by Brad

Klontz, Rick Kahler, and Ted Klontz. National Underwriter Company.

The Small Big: Small Changes That Spark Big Influence (2014) by Steve Martin, Noah Goldstein and Robert Cialdini. Profile Books.

Instant Influence: How to Get Anyone to Do Anything – Fast (2011) by Michael Pantalon. Little, Brown.

For work with couples and families:

How to Give Financial Advice to Couples (2015) by Kathleen Burns Kingsbury. McGraw-Hill.

Intentional Wealth: How Families Build Legacies of Stewardship and Financial Health (2013) by Courtney Pullen. The Pullen Consulting Group.

Money Harmony: A Road Map for Individuals and Couples (2014) by Olivia Mellan and Sherry Christie. Money Harmony Books.

Endnotes

[1] Stone, G. C. (1979), 'Patient compliance and the role of the expert.' *Journal of Social Issues, 35*, pp. 34–59.

[2] World Health Organization (2003), *Adherence to long-term therapies: evidence for action.*

[3] Prochaska, J., Norcross, J., and DiClemente, C. (1995), *Changing for Good, A Revolutionary Six-Stage Program for Overcoming Bad Habits and Moving Your Life Positively Forward.* Avon Books.

[4] Veres writes and speaks extensively on such matters. 'Inside Information', his regular blog for financial service providers, can be found at www.bobveres.com.

[5] Iyengar, S., and Lepper, M. (2000), 'When choice is demotivating.' *Journal of Personality and Social Psychology, 79*, pp. 995–1006.

[6] *Contemplation* and *Action* are two of the stages of change associated with Prochaska et al's transtheoretical model of change in *Changing for Good* (see note 3 above).

[7] This is perhaps as good a place as any to acknowledge the inherent limitations of much of the published research pertaining to the value of financial advice. The two studies mentioned in this paragraph, for example, were designed, funded and reported on by organizations highly committed to promoting the financial planning profession. For an in-depth treatment of the challenges involved in evaluating such research, see Derek Tharp's thoughtful guest post on Michael Kitces' October 4, 2017 blog: 'Can we trust research on the use and benefits of financial advisors?'

[8] Results are discussed in a 2013 study published by the Financial Planning Standards Council, *The Value of Financial Planning.*

[9] *Fidelity Retirement Survey* (2017). Fidelity Canada.

[10] Personal communication with Dan Ariely (2017).

[11] Steffel, M., Williams, E., and Perrmann-Graham, J. (2016), 'Passing the buck: Delegating choices to others to avoid responsibility and blame.' *Organizational Behavior and Human Decision Processes, 135,* pp. 32-44.

[12] Engelmann, J., Capra, C., Noussair, C., and Berns, G. (2009) 'Expert financial advice neurobiologically "offloads" decision-making under risk.' *PLoS ONE, 4 (3),* e4957.

[13] From online article in *Financial Advisor*, December 10, 2013. 'Top 5 Reasons Why Clients Fire Advisors.'

[14] Bernard, J. L., Murphy, M., and Little, M. (1987), 'The failure of clinical psychologists to apply understood ethical principles.' *Professional Psychology: Research and Practice, 18 (5),* pp. 489-491.

[15] A thoughtful examination of these matters is found in Linda Knauss's article, 'Ethics, emotions and values' in the summer 2015 edition of *The Specialist*, a journal of the American Board of Professional Psychology.

[16] Comments made during Heffernan's address to the Financial Planning Association Retreat in Scottsdale, AZ (2012). *Trust: Testing what we think we know.*

[17] All quotes are from Pablo Torre's 2009 *Sports Illustrated* article, 'How (and Why) Athletes Go Broke'. Torre asserts that financially unsophisticated professional athletes often gravitate towards higher-risk investment opportunities such as restaurants, real estate, and retail precisely because those things are easier to understand than

dividends, derivatives and debentures. He refers to this phenomenon as *the lure of the tangible*.

[18] Levitin, D. (2014), *The Organized Mind: Thinking Straight in the Age of Information Overload*, p. 383. Dutton Books.

[19] Meichenbaum, D., and Turk, D. (1987), *Facilitating Treatment Adherence*. Plenum Press.

[20] Online article by Victoria McKeever (2017). 'Behaviour has bigger impact on financial education than facts.' *Professional Adviser*, May issue.

[21] Beckman, H. B. and Frankel, R.M. (1984). 'The effect of physician behavior on the collection of data.' *Annals of Internal Medicine, 101*, 692-696.

[22] Dyche, L, and Swiderski, D. (2005), 'The effect of physician solicitation approaches on ability to identify patient concerns.' *Journal of General Internal Medicine, 20*, 267-270.

[23] In addition to his many scholarly articles and his textbooks on ethics, Ronald Duska writes regular columns for the Society of Financial Services Professionals. I highly recommend his work.

[24] Klontz, B., Kahler, R., and Klontz, T. (2008) *Facilitating Financial Health: Tools for Financial Planners, Coaches, and Therapists*. The National Underwriter Company.

[25] Klontz, Kahler and Klontz are not content to let mental health professionals off the hook, arguing that they should develop as much comfort in dealing with 'Exterior Finance' as advisors should in dealing with 'Interior Finance'.

[26] For a further discussion of how to make warmer connections with people, I recommend the work of Heidi Grant-Halvorson. Start with her 2015 book, *No One Understands You and What to Do about It*. HBR Press.

[27] Johnson, E. (2017), *Working Together in Clinical Supervision: A Guide for Supervisors and Supervisees.* Momentum Press.

[28] Rath, T. and Harter, J. (2010), *Wellbeing: The Five Essential Elements.* Gallup Press.

[29] American Psychological Association, *Stress in America* surveys, 2007–15.

[30] Papp, L., Cummings, E., and Goeke-Morey, M. (2009). 'For richer, for poorer: money as a topic of marital conflict in the home.' *Family Relations, 58,* pp. 91–103.

[31] Wagner, R. (2016), *Financial Planning 3.0: Evolving Our Relationships with Money.* Outskirts Press.

[32] Krueger, D. (2009), *The Secret Language of Money: How to Make Smarter Financial Decisions and Live a Richer Life.* McGraw Hill Education.

[33] Pullen, C. (2013), *Intentional Wealth: How Families Build Legacies of Stewardship and Financial Health,* p. 98. The Pullen Consulting Group.

[34] Mellan, O. and Christie, S. (2014), *Money Harmony: A Road Map for Individuals and Couples.* Money Harmony Books.

[35] Once again, from Pullen's book, *Intentional Wealth* (see above).

[36] Mullainathan, S. and Shafir, E. (2013), *Scarcity: Why Having Too Little Means So Much.* Times Books.

[37] See Cialdini, R. (2016), *Pre-Suasion: A Revolutionary Way to Influence and Persuade.* Simon and Schuster.

Also see Martin, S., Goldstein, N., and Cialdini, R. (2014), *The Small Big: Small Changes That Spark Big Influence.* Grand Central Publishing.

[38] For more information on this phenomenon, read Chip Heath and Dan Heath's book, *Decisive: How to Make Better Choices in Life and Work.*

[39] There are many different approaches to readiness assessment that can be found in the adherence literature, and many variations in the recommended wording of the queries that various researchers suggest using. The Readiness Questions I outline in this chapter are derived from a Pfizer-sponsored Canadian initiative called 3-Minute Empowerment.

[40] Sinek, S. (2009), *Start with Why: How Great Leaders Inspire Everyone to Take Action.* Penguin Group.

[41] For an in-depth discussion of these matters, see Letkiewic, J., Robinson, C., and Domian, D. (2016). 'Behavioral and wealth considerations for seeking professional financial planning help.' *Financial Services Review, 25,* 105-126.

[42] From the Certified Financial Transitionist® training program, a division of the Sudden Money® Institute.

[43] Pullen, *Intentional Wealth*, p. 121.

[44] Personal communication with Kathleen Rehl, June, 2017

[45] Stanny's books include *Overcoming Underearning: A Five-Step Plan to a Richer Life, Prince Charming Isn't Coming: How Women Get Smart About Money,* and *Sacred Success: A Course in Financial Miracles.*

[46] Personal communication, Jim Williams, September, 2017.

[47] More of Dr. Abdulrehman's thoughts about cultural competency can be found on his website, www.leadwithdiversity.com.

[48] Page 27 of Goldsmith's (2015) book, *Triggers: Creating Behavior That Lasts – Becoming the Person You Want to Be.* Crown Business.

[49] Personal communication Dana Hammonds, Senior Director of the NFL Players' Association, September, 2017.

[50] *End of Year Report* (2016). Common Cents Lab, p. 8.

[51] Achor, S. (2013), *Before Happiness: The 5 Hidden Keys to Achieving Success, Spreading Happiness, and Sustaining Positive Change.* Random House.

[52] Baumeister, R. and Tierney, J. (2011), *Willpower: Rediscovering the Greatest Human Strength.* Penguin Press.

[53] Cialdini, R. (2016). *Pre-Suasion: A Revolutionary Way to Influence and Persuade.* Simon and Schuster.

[54] Martha Beck describes such persistent negative experiences as one of the ways in which our 'Essential Self' lets us know whether we're doing the right kind of work. Read more in her 2002 book, *Finding Your Own North Star* (Crown Publications).

[55] One of the best books on the far-reaching benefits of a growth mindset is Carol Dweck's 2006 book *Mindset: The New Psychology of Success* (Random House).

[56] Buechner, F. (1993). *Wishful Thinking: A Seeker's ABC.* Harper One.

Acknowledgements

Writing a book is a lot like other major life projects you might be familiar with: overhauling an engine, renovating a kitchen, delivering a baby. All such projects start out from a place of confidence and enthusiasm, but inevitably include a period of time in the Slough of Despond. If you're going to embark on such an endeavour, it's a really good idea to bring smart and caring people alongside for the journey. It cuts down on the screaming.

My deepest thanks are due to the many companions I've had along the way. Among them:

My colleagues at Thomson House – Darlene, Nina, Karens 1 and 2, Glen, Janine, Brent, and Amanda. You are all exemplars of excellence and kindness in how you care for patients and each other, and you make the clinic a wonderful place to be.

The entire Sudden Money Institute community. You didn't laugh (excessively) when a psychologist stumbled into your midst and asked to know more about your work. You've shared deeply about your experiences and challenges as financial professionals, and been good-natured beta-testers for the materials developed in response to those conversations.

SMI founder Susan Bradley. You continue to be an exceptional friend and mentor. I am beyond grateful for your big mind and even bigger soul.

Ginny Carter, developmental editor and book coach extraordinaire. Thank you for exploring ideas at length while still keeping me on schedule. (And for knowing the perfect time to send me rude videos.)

Graphic designer Brian Hydesmith. Perpetually cheerful, amazingly creative, and picky in all the right ways. How lucky am I to have you as a collaborator AND friend?!

All the folks who read initial drafts of the book – my Mastermind group; my sister, Valerie Somers; and Nazrudin colleagues Rick Kahler, Jim Williams, Steven Shagrin, and Darren Johns. Thanks for wading through the weeds with me.

Publisher Alison Jones, editor Ray Hamilton, and chief book wrangler Abbie Headon. Your attention to detail, your willingness to comb through the intricacies of Canadian vs. American vs. British spellings and terminologies, and your unflagging good humour are just the start of what I appreciate about you.

The menfolk in my life: Jean-Louis, Didier, and Lévi. You've put up with piles of paper, lacklustre cooking, and all-round distractedness for many months. I'll try to make re-entry as painless as possible.

About the Author

Dr. Moira Somers is a clinical neuropsychologist, executive coach, wealth consultant, and professor based in Winnipeg, Manitoba. She could probably be rich if she would just focus on one thing, but she has commitment issues.

Underlying all of these professional endeavours is a fascination with behaviour change. Her career has been devoted to helping people overcome stuckness and resistance – in themselves and/or in the people they serve.

Dr. Somers lives with teenagers and pets that give her plenty of lived experience in the area of non-adherence. Her husband, thankfully, is remarkably well-behaved.

Dr. Somers works with financial professionals around the globe, equipping them to deliver financial advice more effectively. She is available for keynote addresses, workshops, and webinars that are lauded for being science-based, humorous, insightful, and, above all, *practical*. For more information, contact the Arlan Group at arlangroup.com.

Bulk discounts of this book are available to your company, educational institution or conference for re-selling, gifts, or training purposes. For more information, contact the author:

drsomers@moneymindandmeaning.com
or 1 (204) 488-6796

Index

Where your mental energy goes...

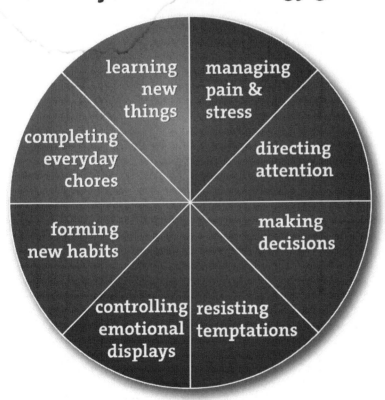